WRITING
THE WORLD

ALSO BY KELLY CHERRY

WRITING
THE WORLD

Kelly Cherry

UNIVERSITY OF MISSOURI PRESS
Columbia and London

University of Missouri Press, Columbia, Missouri 65201
Printed and bound in the United States of America
5 4 3 2 1   99 98 97 96 95

Cherry, Kelly.
   Writing the world / Kelly Cherry.
      p.   cm.
   ISBN 0-8262-0992-0
   1. Cherry, Kelly—Aesthetics.   2. American literature—20th
century—History and criticism—Theory, etc.   I. Title.
PS3553.H357W75   1995
814′.54—dc20   94-49730
                                                                    CIP

∞ This paper meets the requirements of the American National
Standard for Permanence of Paper for Printed Library Materials,
Z39.48, 1984.

Text Design: Elizabeth K. Fett
Jacket Design: Stephanie Foley
Typesetter: BOOKCOMP
Printer and Binder: Thomson-Shore, Inc.
Typeface: Bodoni Book

ACKNOWLEDGMENTS

ESSAYS INCLUDED HERE AND PREVIOUSLY published often appeared under different titles and in versions that have since been revised extensively. "Beginning" was first published in *American Arts* (1981) and was excerpted in *The Manila Chronicle*, Philippines (1992). "Why the Figure of Christ Keeps Turning Up in My Work" was first published in *The Confidence Woman: 26 Women Writers at Work*, edited by Eve Shelnutt (Marietta, Ga.: Longstreet Press, 1991). "Art and Redemption" was first published in *Book Forum* (1982). "Why I Don't Keep a Diary: On Positive Capability" was first published in *Book Forum* (1979). "Why I Am Writing Stories about a Woman Named Nina: Positive Capability Reconsidered" was first published in *Louisiana Literature* (1990). "On Autobiography and Fiction" was first published in *Louisiana Literature* (1992). "Revolution and History: A Topology" was first published in *New Literary History* (1991). "Letter from Latvia: Choosing Independence" was first published in *Chronicles: A Magazine of American Culture* (1992). "A Candle, Burning" was first published in the *PEN Newsletter* (1991). "Poetic Forms as Cartography" was first published with the title "A Flashlight or Map" in *A Formal Feeling Comes: Poems in Form by Contemporary Women*, edited by Annie Finch (Brownsville, Ore.: Story Line Press, 1994). "Watersmeet: Thinking about Southern Poets" was first published in *Book Forum* (1977). "A Conversation around Southern Poetry with Henry Taylor" was first published in *Chronicles: A Magazine of American Culture* (1991). "The World Creating Itself" (in "On Wisconsin!") was first published with the title "On Words" in *American Arts* (1982).

"Faith and Signification" (in "On Wisconsin!") was first published in *The Unicorn* (1983). "Where *Is* the World?" (in "On Wisconsin!") was first published in *American Arts* (1982). "A House in the Desert" was first published in *Jeopardy* (1983). "Writing about Running" was first published in *Willow Springs Magazine* (1983). "The Two Cultures at the End of the Twentieth Century: An Essay on Poetry and Science" was first published in *The Midwest Quarterly* (1994). "Dancing to the Beat of Her Heart" was first published in *Sweet Nothings: An Anthology of Rock and Roll in American Poetry*, edited by Jim Elledge (Bloomington: Indiana University Press, 1994). "Meaning and Music in George Garrett's Fiction" was first published in *The Texas Review* (1989). "Letter from the Philippines: Crossing a Street in Manila" was first published in *Chronicles: A Magazine of American Culture* (1994). "A Brief Encounter with Faulkner" was first published in *Crosscurrents* (1984). "The Place Where There Is Writing" was first published in *The Texas Review* (1985). I am indebted to the editors and publishers of these periodicals and anthologies for the gracious hospitality they have extended to my essays.

For permission to incorporate excerpted material, thanks go also to the authors and publishers of the following works: *An Afternoon of Pocket Billiards*, by Henry Taylor (Baton Rouge: Louisiana State University Press, 1992), copyright © 1992 by the author, used with permission; originally published by the University of Utah Press, 1975. *News of the Nile: A Book of Poems*, by R. H. W. Dillard (Chapel Hill: University of North Carolina Press, 1971), copyright © 1971 by the author, used with permission. *River: A Poem*, by Fred Chappell (Baton Rouge: Louisiana State University Press, 1975), copyright © 1975 by the author, used with permission. *A Paper Horse*, by Robert Watson (New York: Atheneum, 1962), copyright © 1962 by the author, used with permission. *Christmas in Las Vegas*, by Robert Watson (New York: Atheneum, 1971), copyright © 1971 by the author, used with permission. *After Borges: A Sequence of New Poems*, by R. H. W. Dillard (Baton Rouge: Louisiana State University Press, 1972), copyright © 1972 by the author, used with permission. *The Heisenberg Variations*, by John Bricuth (Baltimore: Johns Hopkins University Press, 1981), copyright © 1981 by the author, used with permission; originally published by the University of Georgia Press, 1976. *The New Physics*, by Al Zolynas (Middletown, Conn.: Wesleyan University Press, 1979), copyright © 1979 by the author, used with permission. Poems reprinted from my books *Relativity: A Point of View*, copyright © 1977 by the author, and *Natural Theology*, copyright © 1988 by the author, are used with permission of Louisiana State University Press.

For opportunities to travel and for time to write, I am gratefully obliged to the University of Wisconsin, the Wisconsin Arts Board, the Virginia Center for the Creative Arts, and the Arts America Program of the United States Information Agency. Beverly Jarrett, of the University of Missouri Press, remains an unmet but treasured reader, whose support and encouragement have brightened my publishing life for some years. Last but never least, my colleague Ronald Wallace has been a cheerful and invaluably helpful consultant, generous with his concern for the art.

FOR HENRY, FRED, GEORGE, RICHARD, AND ABE
from the beginning

We shall not cease from exploration . . .

—T. S. Eliot, "Little Gidding," *Four Quartets*

CONTENTS

A NOTE ON PLACE AND PROCESS

THIS BOOK REFLECTS MY NEED to understand what we who are writers actually do when we write and what it may mean to do whatever it is that we do when we write in a particular time and place. I have never written a "travel essay." Travel essays, at least as I think of them, are commissioned; presumably, the travel writer's first obligation is to the contractor of the work. Rather, the essays herein were written for the same reason I always write—a wish to create beauty from a specific kind of knowledge, the knowledge that we acquire by creating beauty. My materials for this task, in this case, were my experiences in various locales. Some of these places, like the Philippines, I was able to visit only briefly; others, like Latvia, have been my heart's compass points. All are places I went to for serious reasons—to make a living, to make a home, to make friends, to become myself. I was not on vacation. I never even set out, as if with an itinerary, to survey all these sites, no more than I set out to be here where I am today, as I am today, in Wisconsin: things happen, and you find yourself living a life here, or there, and you seek to know what it means to be living where you are, and that search is, for a writer, a searching out of language. That *quest* is, for a writer, a *questioning*. For a writer, beauty and knowledge begin in the same place.

A very few of these essays are included more or less as they were first published. Most have been rewritten so extensively that the first printed version may be thought of as a draft. I might have woven some separate essays together, or I might have arranged the

essays chronologically; I chose to do neither. First of all, I wanted
to retain the structural and rhythmic integrity of each essay, which
I had always thought of as a shaped work, not a simple collection of
observations or thoughts. Second, as I approached the book I began
to see it as a long, narrative poem. The individual essays seemed
to me less like chapters, that is, and more like stanzas. There are
recurring lines among these stanzas; there are refrains. *My parents
were string quartet violinists.* And, *We were poor.* Perhaps, in so many
words, *We were allowed to dream.* I liked the echo, the way such
lines act as a kind of base, a place to which we refer—for there is
always a place to which we refer—wherever our lives may take us.
In the end, I moved from essay to essay by a process of association,
letting chronology go hang, so that, I hope, the essays taken together
may be read straight through as a prose poem, a long prose poem
about the world and a writer's place in it.

BEGINNING

I AM A WRITER. I write those words—"I am a writer"—just like that, as if it were as easy as that, or as if it mattered. It has not, in truth, been easy, but it does matter. I *trust* that it matters *literarily*, but I *know* that it matters *literally*. Let me explain.

Tonight I am writing at the kitchen table of a friend's house; the friend is in Iowa. I am here in Madison, Wisconsin, and although I have my own house in this city, I can't afford to live in it; so tenants live in my house, I live in my friend's house, and my friend is in Iowa.

The house in which I am writing is set in the middle of an arboretum; if you don't know to look for it, you're not likely to find it. The postman refuses to deliver packages to the door: too long a hike, too many mosquitoes. I don't mind. I welcome the solitude, the temporary lull in my life. There's a lighted aquarium in the kitchen, and fish swim at my back. I'm lucky to have a friend's house to write in. I sit at the table, drink coffee, and write; my dog, Duncan, barks at raccoons.

The question, then, is not, why do I sit here? but, why do I sit here writing? What earthly purpose does my writing—in the middle of an arboretum in the middle of America—serve?

For a moment, let's set aside the conventional answers. The conventional answers include communication (as of an idea), aesthetic gratification (the reader's, or just the writer's), even art for art's sake. Let's even set aside the work's own demand to be brought into being. All of these are true answers but do not go beyond the specific case, and we're seeking something that goes beyond the specific case. We're seeking something deeper, something broader on which the whole of literature is based, the foundation from which the house of the tradition itself arises.

I am writing in a house in an arboretum in Wisconsin, and you— in your house in South Carolina, your apartment in New York, your office in Chicago or Los Angeles—are reading. This may or may not be an act of communication between us; I hope it is. It may or may not result in aesthetic gratification for one or both of us; I hope it does. And I would probably be writing this piece whether or not it is ever published. But these are effects, not causes. Or let's say they're final causes, but they are not *first* causes. Why does a writer write?

Well, as you can guess from my living arrangements, it's not for money. Some few writers do earn newsworthy incomes, of course; not very many serious ones do, and hardly any innovative ones do. A few more earn sufficient incomes because they were brought along by publishers when the publishing industry was willing to think of an advance not as a down payment on subsidiary rights but as an investment in an author's career; these writers were given time to develop a steady readership. Most of us, if we depended on our writing for an income, couldn't keep body and soul together.

Not long ago, as I was feeling very tired, I decided to figure out how many words I'd written in the past ten years alone. It came to one million finished words, or minimally five to ten million draft words, or one million draft words every one to two years, not counting personal and professional correspondence and research notes. I teach full time. When I teach fiction writing, I average, per semester, three thousand pages of student manuscript to read and mark in sentence-by-sentence detail. That is excluding non-degree students, independent study tutorials, and the odd novel in the anonymous knapsack. Like most writers, I also give readings, serve on panels, do workshops, apply for grants—a series of time-consuming steps that might be called The American Literary Soft-Shoe Shuffle.

Looking at those figures made me proud, but also tireder. I kept thinking how, if I were a different kind of writer, or perhaps Joyce Carol Oates, they would have added up to 730 books, all published, instead of 9½, of which 4 have been published and 5½ are in my desk drawer. But my case—this specific case that is mine—is no different from any other writer's; what I do and experience professionally is no different from what other writers do and experience. This is not just my life; it's a writer's life, and after all, a writer doesn't just choose it; clearly, she does anything she can to be allowed to live it, including—frequently with the secretly compelling sense of being a bit of an adventurer—throwing the rest of her life completely out of alignment.

So. The question returns. Why?

Why does anyone consent to the emotional, financial, spiritual, and even physical contortions that are necessary in order to lead the writer's life in America today? There are almost no grants. (Whether any writers should get grants, and, if so, which writers should get grants, are questions to be addressed elsewhere; here, I am merely reporting on a situation—that is, this situation that most writers will recognize.) Only a few serious writers receive large advances; often, there are no advances at all. But we are blockheads, Dr. Johnson, who would write, who do write, for free! We would give our work away! Yet all too often, manuscripts filed in our desk drawers remain in our desk drawers. We write, most of us writers, without hope of publication or comprehension, happy and grateful when they come but not daring to assume either. We give our lives to our work. Even my dog, who wishes I'd stop this thing I'm doing and come play with him, puts his front paws in my lap and looks up at me, asking, Why?

The answer's as close on the question's heels as Duncan is on mine.

The answer is, *For the same reason I am telling you what my life as a writer is like.*

You had, most probably, no idea who I am; now, like it or not, you're stuck with an idea of me. Not necessarily—though possibly also—an idea of mine, but necessarily an idea of me. You now know that there exists at least one person with the inner dimensions I have described. You may or may not be interested in my life, but that's not the point; and I might have lied—but I haven't—about my life, but neither is that the point. The point is simply that you are now obliged to recognize the writer of this piece as a conscious being. If someday we meet, and shake hands, you can rest assured that I am not some cleverly designed android escaped from a *Star Trek* set. There is another mind in this other body.

We all do this, of course. We are all of us poets and storytellers, making literature of our lives, and when we listen to one another, we learn, through that exercise of the imaginative faculty, that this planet which we at least appear to inhabit is a reality in at least more than one mind. Only the most diehard of Berkeleians would insist that he imagines even the imaginations of other human creatures.

A writer is someone who makes the tracks of her mind's thinking visible for anyone who wants to follow her. This doesn't mean she is limited to autobiography; far from it. Like that stubborn Berkeleian— or like Bishop Berkeley's God—she *can* imagine the imaginations of others, even the imaginations of imaginary people, called characters or personae.

Critics, we may say, are census-takers.

But the writer knows that these imaginary constructs are dependent for their being on language. Therefore she agonizes over her verbs; she frets over her nouns; she restructures her sentences, paragraphs, scenes—and still she can't help knowing that no matter what she finally decides, everything hinges on whether it's Tuesday or Wednesday, and what she ate for breakfast. Does Bishop Berkeley's God struggle with the Divine Syntax?

Tonight, I forgot to mention, is Tuesday night. I sit here writing, and by now it's obvious that the only way I can say I sit *here* writing is *by* writing. Writing locates the *here*, and by unavoidable implication, a *there*.

I stand and stretch, look out the kitchen window. With the porch light on, I can see black oak, white oak, bur oak, black cherry, and shagbark hickory. Arrowwood and elderberry bushes are clumps of shadow; flowering raspberry surrounds the house. Asleep or skittering at the edges of the lawn are possums, foxes, rabbits, woodchucks. I can hear the shy whistle of the phoebe and the evening flute concerto of the woodthrush, and in the distance, the low thrum of Beltline traffic.

I turn back to the kitchen. The lighted fish in the aquarium are living their silent lives. Do you know that the female swordtail has no tail? That, deprived of a mate, she may change her sex?

Black oak, white oak, bur oak, black cherry, and shagbark. These trees, whether or not they grow *really*, in a real arboretum in a real Wisconsin independent of perception, now grow in your brain. I've planted them there; my words are seeds. We are rooted in our language. Whether or not this world exists independently of our consciousness is a question for the idealists and the empiricists still to debate; but your consciousness of my consciousness has unquestionably grown. It buds; it will leaf.

The world, be it real or not, brute fact or gentle illusion, is populated by people who become human through their imaginative awareness of others' inner lives. It is the writer who works hardest to heighten, provoke, prod, even create, germinate and engender that awareness. What joy, what privilege!—to be so essential to existence. This is the writer's earthly purpose and her cause, which she serves gladly, in any circumstances, with a sense of its utter and transcending importance. That's why I said "matters." That's why I said "literally." In the beginning *is* the word.

WRITING
THE WORLD

Why the Figure of Christ
Keeps Turning Up in My Work

MY SISTER THINKS I SHOULDN'T LET anyone know what our childhood was like. "It was not a normal childhood," she says. "It's better not to talk about it. It's better not to *think* about it." She says she is ashamed of our childhood and that she feels other people would look at us strangely if they knew about it.

Nevertheless, we were not mistreated the way, one notes sorrowfully, so many children are. No, it was simply that, for long periods of time—for years on end—our parents were distracted, and forgot that we were around.

My sister has a clearer memory for these years than I do; I was a dreamy kid, as distracted by my own thoughts as my parents were by theirs. "Don't you remember," my sister asks me, "that we were not even taught to brush our teeth until we went to school? The school nurse was shocked."

I reply that our parents undoubtedly thought there was no point in worrying about baby teeth that were destined to fall out.

"For one cold winter in the country," she goes on, referring to the year after we had moved away from the tenement flat in upstate New York, "I had no mittens because nobody noticed that I needed a pair."

I do remember that winter. The furnace didn't run, and my sister and I were not allowed to turn on the kerosene heater. After school, she and I would huddle together under our coats in the scratchy upholstered armchair, listening to "Sergeant Preston of the Yukon" and other radio shows until our parents got home from work.

We were kids on the loose, kids at large. The neighbors told my parents that I was a "child of nature," and my parents thought this was a scream and teasingly repeated the epithet to me, never realizing that what the neighbors meant by it was that my hair needed combing.

What had consumed their attention so, leaving them little to give to their children's socialization, was music. They were string quartet violinists. But this is not to say that our family lived a life of intellectual glamour and elegance. Despite people's notions of string quartets and string quartet playing, it is possible to be a string quartet player in the same way that a poet is likely to be a poet: poor, and taking on other kinds of work to make the poetry possible. My parents were poor and took on other kinds of work to make their string quartet playing possible. Not until their later years did my parents enter the ranks of the economically middle class, and even then they were always afraid some financial disaster would, without warning, catapult them back out of it.

There were *moments* of glamour and elegance, though, and more important, there were whole days and nights of the most astonishing beauty imaginable—right there in the living room, where my parents and the violist and the cellist were making the room blue with smoke. There was an ashtray on every footstool and a footstool beside every player. There was a cup of cocoa on my mother's footstool and a cup of coffee on everybody else's footstool. Nobody ever used a footstool as a footstool. My parents' music stands were black iron, heavy as armament; the violist's and cellist's music stands would be the aluminum ones that you can fold up and carry to rehearsal. My parents had these music stands too, for when they went elsewhere to play. When they went elsewhere, my sister and I were again kids on the loose, kids at large. (We were also kids with the music of Beethoven in our hearts and on our minds.)

They worked so hard, our parents did, what with trying to earn enough money to get by and then practicing and rehearsing and performing on top of that, that even if they had wanted to—and really, they didn't want to—they had no time or energy to think about us. And if they couldn't be bothered to teach us how to comb our hair or brush our teeth, they certainly couldn't be bothered to teach us religion. We never went to church. Who had time to go to church? Moreover, who would *want* to go to church and have to say hello to people? My parents didn't much like people. People were dumb bosses, busybody neighbors, and other undesirable two-legged creatures.

As for God, my mother, at least, had her doubts. She felt that the only goodness in the historical world had been accomplished by a handful of exceptional beings, most of them composers or artists or scientists (writers had a perverse predilection for focusing on the ugliness of the world). So far as she could see, if there was a God, he wasn't a very smart one. Or he was cruel, causing suffering in a way that at least looked malicious and, if it wasn't that, was at best callous. She felt some guilt about harboring these doubts—she knew that her mother and father in Mississippi would have been distressed by them and, even more discomfitingly, might feel sorry for her for having to endure them—but she was a tough-minded thinker with a deep distaste for people's ability to fool themselves. People *were* foolish. People would settle for anything, even Bruckner.

The one time we visited our grandparents in Gulfport, Mississippi, my sister and I were spirited off to the Presbyterian church, where we were given a copy of the Shorter Catechism and told to memorize it. *What is man's chief end? Man's chief end is to glorify God, and to enjoy Him forever.* I remember the cool stone walls of the church, lilies and irises heaped at the altar, the satiny polished wood of the pews, fans like Ping-Pong paddles, and hymnals with their lovely thin pages waiting in the pockets of the backrests.

What is man's chief end? It is to glorify God and to enjoy Him forever.

I thought these words were wonderful—although to be honest, I was even more impressed with my ability to recite the Catechism. (There were 107 questions and answers.) Perhaps it was the first time that my demonstrated ability to do something, as differentiated from my potential to fulfill parental fantasies of success, had been important to anyone. Perhaps I just liked the process of learning, the way I had liked learning how to spell *sulfanilamide*, saying the syllables over and over, pleased as punch by their phonetic charm.

We had moved back down South before I had another encounter with religion. It was the year I turned ten. For my birthday, my grandmother, who clearly thought that the Shorter Catechism was but a beginning, sent me a Bible. It was the King James Version, it had a black, grained cover and a zipper, and because it was the first book I had ever owned by myself, I thought I should read it. And so I did, working my way through the *begat*s to Job, and on to the major and minor prophets, and onward still to the New Testament, not skipping a word because skipping would be cheating, right up to Mark 16:16, which so offended me that I drew a blue-ink box around the verse and stared and stared at it: "He that believeth and is baptized shall be saved; but he that believeth not shall be damned." I still have this Bible—which, however, my dog ate a good part of a few years ago, becoming thereby, I should think, an unusually holy dog, eucharistic in the extreme—and when I open it to Mark I find that blue-ink square, drawn in a ten-year-old hand.

Enraged, I carried the Bible downstairs. My parents were sitting in the kitchen. "Read this," I commanded, and they obeyed.

"Well?" they asked, lifting their eyebrows. (My father was handsome, and my mother was beautiful, and my father could lift one eyebrow at a time.)

"It's a bribe!" I said. "I don't think this is right! If you're good you go to heaven, and if you're bad you go to hell. But you ought to want to be good without being promised a heaven, and you ought to want not to be bad without being threatened with a hell."

As I remember it, that is very close to what I actually said.

I am sure that my parents thought this, too, was a scream.

At the same time, they were the kind of people who worry about such things, and so a debate ensued on whether heaven and hell were bribe and threat or merely the consequences of one's behavior, assuming that heaven and hell existed, which they probably didn't, because if they did they weren't working very well to keep things in order on earth and if they existed there would have to be a God but if there were a God you'd think He could come up with a better idea, one that would work. I finished reading the Bible—it would have been cheating not to—but I was skeptical. I had written a story titled "Tiny Angelcake," about an angel named Angelcake (whom everyone called Pieface). Pieface wanted to take a present to the baby Jesus lying in a manger in Bethlehem, but was short on funds. On the way there he met The Three Wise Men. "What," said The Three Wise Men, "are you doing here?"

"Going to see the Messiah," answered the angel.

"Keeping up with the news! Ha, ha, ha!" They laughed and went on their way.

When Pieface got to the manger where Jesus lay, he found he still had nothing to give Him, so he composed a poem, of which I remember that two lines went something like this:

> For thou art the Son of God
> Even though many things He does to us seem very odd.

But we were living in the Bible Belt now, and the next year we moved closer to town. There was a man in the house next to ours who said everything wrong—the rose bushes, he complained, were being attacked by *asps*—and across the back way there lived a divorcée in a large ramshackle house with a mulberry tree in the side yard. At one end of the block that our house was on there was a combination lunchroom and beer joint. And at the other end of the block there was a woman who invited the neighborhood children to come to her house after school to hear stories from the New Testament. I had been rejected by the Brownies—"We think your daughter will be happier in some other organization," the women who led the troop told my mother—and I was relieved to find that the invitation included me. We sat on the floor. She had cutouts of the Bible characters that she moved around on a green felt board. Somehow the colorful figures adhered to the board. The figures' robes were bright, and some of the figures carried staffs or jugs of wine and water, and there were houses and sheep, and children too, all living in a place that was always sunny. When I had a chance to go to Bible summer school, I quickly agreed, riding the bus every day into the city. There, at the church, I learned to make a beanie.

When our neighborhood church started its own Vacation Bible School, I was, therefore, ready. I had never been to church in this church, but I knew what to expect from Vacation Bible School. This time I learned to make a purse. It was white, and it had a rope handle that you pulled on to make the purse open and shut. But this Bible school didn't last for long, because the preacher, whose wife taught the purse-making class, had knocked up the neighborhood divorcée.

As a fiscally if not morally responsible preacher, he had saved some money to support the divorcée during her confinement, but instead she left town to have her baby. In her absence, to redeem his reputation, the preacher held a week-long revival in a large tent near the mulberry tree.

Figuring he'd better not harp on the evils of sex, he opted for the evils of alcohol. Night after night he harangued the penitent. As for the unrepentant, "This very night," he shouted, "God in His wrath may strike dead some sinner who, instead of being here at this revival, is sitting on a barstool in a beer joint!"

While the preacher was uttering these words, a young man sitting on a barstool in the beer joint at the end of the block that our house was on keeled over with a heart attack. The next night the preacher had two new converts—Ike and Ida, the proprietors of the tavern.

"We want to dedicate our lives to Christ," Ida declared.

"We'd stop selling beer right now," Ike, who wore an *I Like Ike* button, explained, "and just run a lunchroom, but we don't know what to do with the twenty cases of beer we have stored in the pantry."

The preacher promised to give the matter careful consideration. The next morning, he'd come up with a solution. He drove to the tavern, bought all the beer that was stored in the pantry, and loaded it in the back of his old station wagon. That night, at the revival meeting, he told the congregation how Ike and Ida had been born again and how he had used his savings to buy all the beer in the pantry to free them from temptation. "Saturday afternoon," he announced, "there will be a picnic near the bridge at Rattlesnake Creek. You are all invited. There will be sandwiches and soft drinks, and the beer'll be poured into the creek." And then he added, "Hallelujah!"

Well, everyone was so impressed that the collection plate over-flowed, and for days thereafter contributions came in via the mails. There was enough money for a new station wagon, which Mrs. Preacher drove when she did her grocery shopping.

Ike and Ida stayed saved, but before long there was another beer joint at the other end of Jahnke Road, just a little farther down from the house where I used to go to hear Bible stories. And what, oh what, I wonder now, became of the divorcée and her love child?

Even though my family didn't go to church, or attend revivals, living in the Bible Belt I heard a good deal of talk about God. Finally, when I was twelve, I went to my mother. "What do you think about all this?" I asked. "Do you believe in God?"

She answered me by putting a record on the turntable. It was a late Beethoven quartet. "I don't know whether or not there's a God," she said, "but I know there was a Beethoven, and that's good enough for me."

It set high standards, this love of Beethoven did—and the love of Bach—and yet I would not for anything trade the years of being enthralled by this music and of trying to fathom it: of trying to understand what it was saying and of trying to figure out how to *say*, in words, what it was saying. I wrote a long "Letter to Myself" in which I vowed that I would never forget what it *really* meant to be an artist, any artist. What it really meant, I believed, was to listen to the deepest soundings of the heart and the most elevated commandments of the soul and encode these discoveries in the eternal, communicative forms of art. I don't suppose I had any idea of how this might be done, but I believed it was what one had to do. To tell the truth, I even believed it was what one had been born to do.

In those days, however, even if you had been born to do it, you could not do it in college. If you were female, the presumption was that you would not do it even after college until, say, you were well married or established in a "real" profession and had time on the side to mess around with something a little more fanciful, except that by then you'd have outgrown these romantic notions. If my parents knew enough to know that even girls, even Southern girls, could be deeply serious about their artistic ambitions, they were that much more bitter about the hard life that went with such ambitions and that much more determined to steer their elder daughter in a different direction. I shortly found myself, for example, studying math and science, often in unexpected places like the New Mexico Institute of Mining and Technology.

In the absence of writing classes—for there were none at the schools I attended—I had dreamed of permission to major in philosophy. I had dreamed of this permission from the age of fourteen, and I got it in my last year, after six transfers to five schools, two of which I'd been kicked out of; and I got it after a six-month respite dictated by the fact that we could find no college anywhere that would have me, during which period my mother kept telling me I now had two choices in life: My math credits qualified me to be a Grade 4 civil servant. Or I could go to a place in Florida where I would be trained to run a motel. (The magazines, at this time, were full of ads for these schools where you could learn how to run a motel. Our nation had fallen in love with the idea of taking vacations, with the idea of being able to *drive* to vacation, with the idea of a vacation *being* driving.)

During that six-month enforced stay out of school, I read, in *Time* magazine, which was the closest I'd ever gotten to a literary periodical, about a French girl named Françoise Sagan, who had published a novel. This was the first clue I had that books could be written by live female people. I had previously thought that becoming a writer worked like this: First, you studied a subject that would help you to get a job. Next, you got the job, and, while taking care of a husband and children, and working, you wrote a book. Eventually you grew old, and no doubt tired, too, and you died, and then the book was published. Probably, along the way, somewhere in between your writing the book and its getting published posthumously, you also suffered a sea change and became male.

I was the same age as Sagan—eighteen—so I followed her example and wrote a novella, encouraged by visions of reviews in *Time*. But I didn't understand that what made her book newsworthy was not just her age but her subject matter, sex. I didn't know very much about sex and what I did know about it didn't seem very literary to me. Instead, for one hundred pages, I narrated the rediscovery of the Ten Commandments after the nuclear holocaust of World War III. The protagonist vaguely resembled Moses. There was a dead silver crow that functioned as a crucifixion image—the title was *The Silver Crow*. I guess I thought I knew a little something about religion, though looking back, I am not sure that I did not know more about sex.

This novella failed to make me famous but it did convince my parents to give up on the science idea and let me major in philosophy. I loved the rigor of philosophy, the hardcore up-against-the-wall cut-the-crap kind of philosophy that looked on philosophy of religion or political philosophy or aesthetics with disdain. But I also, secretly, loved philosophy of religion and political philosophy and aesthetics. I read Aquinas and Augustine, and briefly consulted with a Dominican priest, but I couldn't consent to the hierarchical structure of Catholicism, its sacerdotal bias—all those men with catechistic answers to questions I preferred to ask for myself—and, too, my aesthetic propensities were for white-frame churches or churches with cool stone walls bare of ornament. Also, I didn't believe in God.

By the time I left graduate school, I realized why my parents had been so eager for me to become a scientist. All my work in philosophy qualified me for a job at sixty dollars a week as an editorial assistant for the Presbyterian Board of Christian Education in Richmond. I was still paying rent on the empty apartment in Charlottesville because the landlady wouldn't let me out of my lease, and my parents were good Calvinists who wouldn't have dreamed of letting me just not pay.

Despite the low pay—young men with my qualifications were earning five times as much—this was a great job. I got to spend all day reading the Bible and the dictionary. I worked at the Board from eight in the morning till four-thirty in the afternoon. At four-thirty, I went to my nighttime job, where until eleven I typed addresses on envelopes (later, I was promoted to the position of writing fake histories for overseas orphans whose real histories were unknown, so that their stateside sponsors would feel closer to them). On weekends I freelanced, writing the script for a biblical filmstrip, or revising church literature so that it could be recorded for the blind. I wrote my poems and stories during lunch hour, in the ladies' room. Working this way, I managed to save enough money to go to Europe, and when I came back from Europe, I entered a graduate program in creative writing—I had not known before that there were any such programs—and was for the first time wholly happy in school, and then, because at twenty-five I was an old maid, but also because he was marvelously intellectually exciting, a thrilling person to talk with, I married a sculptor who had come down from New York City to teach for one semester. He was Jewish, and his family disowned him for marrying me. The wedding took place over the Christmas holidays, and there was a Christmas tree in the living room, but we made sure to omit any reference to Christ in the service, and we put a Moslem ornament on the top of the tree—but his parents still refused to be present, and they wrote him out of the will.

My in-laws might have liked for me to convert, but I was much too stubborn to do something like that just to please people I hadn't even met—they declined to meet me—and, of course, as I now see, if I had converted I would have obviated the point my husband was making by marrying me. No, I didn't consider conversion until *afterward*—after the marriage had ended, after the divorce. We had been living in New York, and after our divorce, I stayed on there, taking on a variety of jobs. One of them was writing an analytic teacher's guide to a collection of Jewish morality tales for a Judaica publishing house. I had protested to the publisher that I knew nothing about Jewish morality tales, but he was unfazed. He sat me down at a small typing table two feet away from his own desk, so there was no way I could not do the work that had been set before me, which was to think about certain stories from the Torah and the Midrash and the Talmud and so forth and try to understand them. And plainly, this was another wonderful job. It would have been grand to have had the access to early publication that writers have now, to have had celebrity teachers who could hand me over to their agents or refer me to writers' colonies, to have had time off with the aid of literary grants, and I would never undervalue the sense of professionalism and, often, the self-confidence that the structure of today's literary world promotes, but if I had had those things

I would have missed out not only on the amazing teachers I did have but also on several years of deep involvement with theological tradition. I might never have learned how to sit still at a typing table and *think*—and my boss *always* knew when I wasn't *thinking*. He seemed not in the least to mind that my interpretation of these Jewish morality tales was markedly Calvinist. There is a generation of children who went to synagogues on Long Island and grew up on my Calvinist interpretations of Jewish morality tales.

One weekend something happened to me that upset me greatly. I called my boss and said that I would not be able to come in to work because I planned to kill myself. (And I meant it.) "Let's have lunch first," he said, "at Max's Kansas City."

Seated in the booth, I told him what had happened. "What a wonderful story that would make," he said. "Write it."

"Oh no, I'll never ever write anything again," I said. I had not written anything in a long time, having concluded from certain life experiences, not to mention my husband's restrictive opinions of women in general, that a woman's wanting to write, or at least my wanting to write, *was* a romantic notion. I was completely without any kind of confidence in myself, whether about writing or anything else, and every morning the first thing I did upon waking was remind myself that I was *not* a writer and must not presume to be one.

"Then don't write a story," he said. "Write me a letter. Just put in it exactly what you've told me today."

So I wrote my boss, whom I hardly knew, a letter. And rewrote it and rewrote it. I wrote it over a dozen times, and then I gave it to him. It was still only about sixteen pages long. "This is interesting," he said. "I'm going to show it to my friend the writer."

He had a friend who was a writer, and he let this friend use one of the company desks and a typewriter and telephone every day. He carried my letter to his friend, who, a half-hour later, came into our room and said, "You need a scene here and here and here." And he made little X's in the right-hand margin everywhere he thought I needed a scene.

I worked on the story for the next six months, and when it was done, at something over forty pages, I took it in to the office. The friend said, "Now send this to—" and he named a prestigious magazine published by a Jewish organization. I had not sent my work out before, though a few things had found their way into publication, and I sent the story where he told me to send it. It came back by return mail. The editor had attached a note. "If you want to know why I rejected this," the note said, "call my secretary."

"Call his secretary," the friend said.

"I can't!"

"You can use the telephone in here," my boss said.

So I called the editor's secretary, and in a few hours a messenger arrived with a slip of paper on which several questions had been noted in pencil. As I remember, they were rather broad: "What does the title mean? Why does the story end the way it does?"

I was sure that what I was supposed to do now was give up. "No, no, no," the friend said. "What you are supposed to do now is wait three weeks, reread the story, make the changes that it will then be apparent to you are needed, and send the story back."

"Send it back? After it's been rejected? Won't he think I'm pestering him?"

But I did what the friend said, and three weeks later I discovered that the editor's questions, though broad, had been precisely to the point. This time I heard not by return mail, not by messenger—the phone rang, and it was the editor, and he was accepting my story, which made use of the idea of covenant and commented on many odd things that seemed to have been done to humankind.

"The only thing is," he said, "there are too many obscenities in it. You'll have to cut some."

Well, I went to work cutting obscenities. I cut every obscenity I thought I could cut and sent the story back to the editor. He telephoned a second time. "You've cut too many obscenities," he said. "We'll have to put some back."

By this time, my boss was making me use the telephone in the showroom. We had an ecumenical showroom, and there were nuns browsing among the books, and a rabbi or two eating lunch from paper bags at the long table. The editor, at his end of the line, and I, at my end of the line, proceeded to have a thoroughly filthy conversation discussing which of the original dirty words should be restored. And when the story came out, with all these dirty words, I went to the dry cleaner's to pick up my dry cleaning, and the tailor looked at the name on his slip and said, "I just read your story! Let me call my wife!" And he called, "Queenie, come here!" and his wife appeared from behind a curtain, and they both shook my hand, and I signed the receipt for him as an autograph, and he handed over my dry cleaning and I walked home so full of confidence I was ready to burst with it. I had confidence to spare, confidence to give to all and sundry.

I had begun attending a conversion class. I was the only member of the class who was neither engaged nor recently married to a Jew, but as I say, it was only after I'd been divorced from a Jew that I felt I could legitimately consider converting to Judaism. There was much in the tradition that attracted me, and I completed the class with every expectation of going through the conversion ceremony. And then something happened: I realized I could *not* go through with it. I realized that what had been propelling me along this particular course was a political sympathy, a sense that in an unjust world the only just act is to align oneself with the victims of injustice. If we were not part of the solution, we were part of the problem.

But when class was over, and I held my certificate in my hand and it was time to convert, I found, welling up in me, a hitherto unrecognized attachment to, of all unexpected things, the figure of *Christ*. I could not let go of this figure that had, all unknown to me, become a part of my deepest self. In fact, it was the figure of Christ that, to me, explained my attraction to Judaism. Here was the emotional heart of my passion for justice.

I still didn't believe in God. God, you see, was never what any of this was about . . .

I put the certificate, which I still treasure, in a footlocker with other treasures (mostly early manuscripts, some photographs and letters, a valentine from my husband, when he had been my husband), and started trying to figure out what this *was* about. In a long poem titled "A Bird's-Eye View of Einstein," I tried to grasp the idea of the Trinity—the mathematical mystery of three-in-one—by stealing a tack from the theory of relativity. I built the poem in three parts, naturally, interpreting the Son or Bridegroom through my ex-husband, the Holy Ghost through my brother, and God the Father through my father; where relativity comes in is that I let my point of view slide in a rather peculiar way through all three parts, bending the time of the poem back on itself. Though the plan of triads is carried out extensively—there are mini-sermons alluding to the three major prophets of the Old Testament (Jeremiah, Ezekiel, Isaiah), dramatizations of the breaking of the three Freudian taboos (cannibalism, incest, murder), and so on through strata of trinities—it was the linking of them through point of view that was what the poem was about. And that linkage culminated in an image of the crucifixion— rather, to be frank, a brutal image, in which the narrator's murderous complicity is made clear, as well as the narrator's self-abnegation in favor of the very thing she has destroyed.

It was a perilously difficult poem to write, demanding as much concentration as I was capable of and so painful that I frequently wept and then had to write on spiral notebook pages that were wet and that smeared the ink. I wrote it while I was teaching at a university in southwest Minnesota, during the break between quarters. I wrote it at night, through the night, emerging into the morning light blinded and monomaniacal. With the students gone, with snow on the ground for as far as the eye could see—and the eye could see very far in that flat, beautiful but desolate landscape—I was cut loose from the world, as if I had been cast into outer space. I would shut the door to my office, and it was like going into a space capsule that would carry me to constellations of thought and feeling that had previously seemed unreachable or whose existence I had not even suspected. Night after night I read The Gospel According to St. John and The Book of Revelation, and it was a revelation to me how inextricably bound I was to this figure of the abandoned Christ and how much responsibility I felt I bore for things gone wrong, love ungranted. For love unfulfilled in action, and for wrongdoing that inhibits right doing. I learned, with the force of pure feeling, just what crimes I was capable of, and it was out of this struggle with myself that I made this poem about the crucified Christ. In the end, it was, perhaps, less a conventionally Christian poem than a poem of eternal recurrence, a stoic acknowledgment of the eternal cycle of despair and hope, sin and redemption, grief and triumph.

In an autobiographical narrative, *The Exiled Heart*, in which I try to know what I can about the nature of freedom and the meaning of love—a task I had set myself because I was engaged to a Latvian composer I had met in Moscow on that first trip to Europe—but Brezhnev's KGB prevented our marriage—I found myself turning again to the figure of Christ, crucified and risen, as a way to think about these subjects. Even now it would be difficult for me to say that I believe in God, even the most sophisticatedly defined kind of God. I was raised to be a doubter, and I'll go on doubting until I can put my hands through holes. But here is the thing: the issue of belief, for me, I now see, is a *secondary* one. I have finally figured out that *belief* is the question that arises in the *middle* of the discourse, and the discourse itself is Christ. I have figured out that the language I think with, the language I have thought with since I first began to think, is the figure of Christ. "In the beginning was the Word, and the Word was with God, and the Word was God." It is through the figure of Christ that I have come the closest to saying what I want to say—what I believe I have heard music saying to me. This is not to say that I think or write only about the figure of Christ. Obviously not. But the figure of Christ is central to everything I write, whether it is there on the page or not. It is the "word" I write with, even when it is not the word I write. In the Logos we have been given a language that can speak the silences, that can say what we may not dare say otherwise, a language that allows us to think about every aspect of the world, human and inhuman, about even those aspects that might otherwise frighten us into the silence of children without parents, which is what we all, ultimately, are—left alone, forgotten. I would not for one minute say it is the only language, but it is my language, my native language.

Still, as I write these words, I can hear someone objecting to the—what do we say?—the maleness of this language. I hear that feminist chorus that would rather say *goddess* than *god*, that finds a male Christ insufficiently androgynous. I am sympathetic to the sense of disenfranchisement that these voices seek to correct, but for myself, it is exactly that maleness that I am unwilling to give up: I want a language that lets me think beyond myself. I want a language through whose agency I am able to transcend my own hungry ego. I want a wider view of the world than I can obtain only through my own eyes. I want to know the Other. I want, that is, to be a *writer*. In this respect, I sometimes think, I may actually be more fortunate than men writers today. The ground of female being is a territory less literarily charted than the ground of male being. A woman writer, if she has an adventurous spirit, can go anywhere, and almost everywhere she goes will be a new and subtle place, rich in unexplored implications, epiphanous, unexhausted. She can *translate* herself, as it were, to places the reader has never been, or does not yet realize he has been.

She can say what it is like to have been there.

And if she does, she will be dedicated to a purpose that is chief, glorious, and joyful forever. At least, this is what I believe. I believe that we *must* say all that it is within our power to say, and we *must* think about all that it is within our power to think about. Our lives, let us say, are sentences, life sentences, surrounded by a silence so profound that it is tautological, a preface and an epilogue of pure silence. We speak them, and they are uttered against such a silence as is terrifying, and salutary, to contemplate.

Art and Redemption

WE WERE POOR. Not dirt poor, I must admit, nor ghetto poor, but just about. We were poor enough, that is, to worry where the next meal was coming from. Luckily, our parents had a sense of humor—it favored the absurd but certainly did not dismiss the ironic—and the fact that we lived three flights above a grocery store gave us something to laugh about at dinner time. Oh, we did eat: hot dogs and Hershey bars, mostly. Vegetable soup when the tomatoes in the bins downstairs began to turn spotty.

We were poor, but we owned one object of very great value. It was a J. B. Guadagnini. And this was another irony: if it had not been for the Great Depression, my father would never have been able to buy this violin. Because of the depression, even violin dealers were operating on slim margins, and my father, inventing the installment plan on the spot, talked one of them into letting him buy the Guadagnini on time.

(The dealer was rather pleased with himself. In March, 1947, William Lewis and Son, the well-known establishment in Chicago, became positively effusive—as violin dealers, a formal lot, go—in a letter to my father. "The writer too is very happy," exclaimed a Mr. H. Benson in behalf of the firm, "and rejoices with the Cherry family that your account for the Guadagnini is paid in full. We know that it has been quite a struggle for you at times and we believe that we have done our share in seeing that you kept the instrument." This letter hangs in a frame on my living-room wall.)

Both of my parents were violinists, or as violinists refer to themselves, fiddle-players. They were always one half of a string quartet.

Of the children, my sister became the musician; but even I, for example, though it's an early talent since lost, could sing in time and on key before I could walk or talk. My parents loved, more than anything else in the world, the late Beethoven quartets. We, the children, listened to them practice. They practiced on snowy days and through long, dimly lit evenings; they practiced in the summer when the sound of kids' roller skates scraping along the cement sidewalks rose to our flat, and they practiced all during one Easter vacation when I lay in bed with the measles, window shades drawn against the sun—lay listening to Beethoven and hugging tightly the ridiculous, magnificent, long-necked toy goose someone had given me.

All this was in Ithaca, but we'd come up from the deep South. My father had been at Louisiana State University for many years, and we'd survived the depression better than many. One thing Huey Long did was make sure that no one on his faculty got cut. They didn't always get paid, or they got paid in scrip, but they didn't get cut.

The depression had made my parents money-shy (money was not trustworthy), but the real source of their perpetual anxiety was not the stock market. It was not the war, because my father, who had gone immediately to the recruiting center, was deemed too old, too hostage to parental responsibilities, and much too nearsighted. No, the real source was, of all things, music. I knew this even by the time we moved north to Ithaca, and I was only four then. I had parents who, when they were young, believed in starving for art. When we moved north to Ithaca, it was not for money but for art.

What we did for *money* was type menus.

My mother would stay up well past midnight night after night typing the menus for the greasy spoon across the street. In the morning, I delivered them to the greasy spoon's owner, leaping down stairs from landing to landing. It amazed me that the words in my hands all spelled "food."

> If food is scarce, feed
> on your own tongue;
> what words bleed?

If poetry begins in wonder, one originating wonder is what we experience when we realize how little relationship words bear to

reality. I could read and reread each day's menu; it bore absolutely
no connection to what did or didn't appear on our plates at night.
I realize that it is the wisdom of the age to say that poets create
by naming, that—this must mean—they call the world forth into
comprehensible being by naming, but poets who think, know well they
can name and name and name, and not one new thing comes into
being. The words multiply; the fishes and loaves won't even swell.

No, the words themselves wouldn't appear on our plates, wouldn't
fill our stomachs. They were merely tokens—and what they signified
had to be purchased by other tokens: coins.

As soon as I figured that out, I hitched a string from one end of
my room to the other, making a dividing line that could be crossed
only upon payment of a toll. Since my sister was the only person who
ever had any need or the slightest desire to cross to my side of our
bedroom, it was she from whom I gathered my first riches. She, of
course, had to get them somewhere else first. She was a devastatingly
cute kid, with huge bark-brown eyes flecked with green and yellow.
She had a tiny nose, blonde bangs, a crazy smile. At one point, we
called her Wiggletail, after a Golden Book about a puppy. On the
other hand, I looked like a young thug. I wore wool trousers and a
long-sleeved pale blue shirt that I was convinced was silk though it
could not have been and a beret—I was convinced it was a beret,
though it was more like a cap with ear flaps—and, at eight, I scowled
constantly. We worked out a system whereby I picked wildflowers in
the gorge, Cascadilla Gorge, and she, as the more appealing one,
sold them to strolling Cornell couples. Working her own end of the
stick, she refused to split more than sixty-forty, so that she always
had more money than I did, until such time as she needed to get to
the toy chest, which was on my side of the room.

While my parents were practicing Beethoven, my sister and I were
learning how to rip each other off.

But we listened, even when we were playing Cash Register and
Toll Troll. Even when we were so cold and hungry we agreed to
pretend the string wasn't there and snuggled up to keep each other
warm and told stories. Golden Books had nothing on me. For I, after

all, was the one who told the stories; my sister, as I say, became the musician, and currently is *starving for art.*

Maybe writers are always more mercenary than musicians. In any case, after a good many years of writing, I began to discover that one theme that was obsessive with me was money. The first long series of poems I did was about an economics professor, although his being an *economics* professor is given out only in one throwaway reference to John Maynard Keynes. Which is perhaps the best way to refer to John Maynard Keynes.

My first novel dealt in considerable part with the moral obligations of employee to employer (yes, that way around), especially when the employer is rich; my second used blackmail as a fulcrum for farce, and the idiom *to pay attention* as a metaphor for love, and in particular for communication in marriage. A third novel is about revolution; that is, about the problems of distribution of wealth (and naturally, it is a comedy). I am, furthermore, the sort of person who overpays her taxes. I envision God as a sort of IRS agent, and it is only the suspicion that IRS agents envision themselves as God that helps me to keep things in perspective.

But is it so farfetched to think of God as the Great Collector in the Sky? You remember Numbers 18:15—

> Every thing that openeth the matrix in all flesh, which they bring unto the LORD, whether it be of men or beasts, shall be thine: nevertheless the firstborn of man shalt thou surely redeem, and the firstling of unclean beasts shalt thou redeem.

God is talking to Aaron and the Levites. In ancient Judaea, the eldest son was meant to be an offering to Yahweh; he could be redeemed from service in the synagogue only by the payment of a sum, which the father supplied. Rightfully, the son *belonged to God;* his father could only *buy him back.* I am no biblical scholar, but a hunch tells me that even before the son was required to be redeemed, a lamb—food—was bought back the same way. I'd *bet* on it. Did God eat? The people, at least, had to.

Possibly the story of Abraham and Isaac hearkens back to such a time.

It is an odd but tough and satisfying notion to think that the son is to be saved from God's jaws. This suits us better than the thought of old Kronos devouring his children. We want to serve God, but not too well—and not fresh meat.

So the son is snatched from death-in-life. And re-enters time.

"I write to redeem lost time, lived time, to buy time back from the High Priest of Death. Any less passionate, despairing, catholic, or economical use of words seems to me sentimental, lacking humor." Somebody had asked me to make a statement about why I write, and so I did, though all such statements are doomed to a kind of inflation. I meant the part about humor, though; meant it as much as—let's face it—I meant the rest of it. The writer, you see, can't buy time back *the way it was;* she can only buy it back *the way it will be forever.*

(And even that's assuming the paper they so often print on these days doesn't disintegrate in fifty years.)

The writer buys back the *future*—and tells herself, tries to convince herself, that it is the *past* she has redeemed; and knows she has failed, and tries again, goes for broke—and goes broke: heartbroke.

The fishes and loaves won't even swell.

Clearly, neither coins nor words quite do the trick. Lives? A New Testament God, more tenderhearted than any revenuer, gives up *his* son to redeem the world from the wages of sin. But your life won't accomplish that—nor mine. Our lives just aren't worth that much. They may be infinitely precious, but they aren't *infinitely* precious.

Yet there is one thing we possess that is that precious, one thing with an equivalent exchange rate: *memory.* Memory brings back the past. And so I treasure the memory I have of that Guadagnini. The Guadagnini itself is still in fine shape—fit as a fiddle—but here we are talking about my memory of it. Purchased before I was born, that fiddle is, to me, as much a part of the creation as the heavens and the earth, and certainly State Street.

That fiddle has a tone so brilliant that when my father drew his bow across the strings, every otherwise dull and secondhand object in the apartment, from the flip-side toaster to the spindle on the turntable of the 78-speed record player, gleamed as if newly polished. This is a fiddle that hushed all city sounds; I think the kids stopped roller-skating just to hear its glorious voice. In fact, I caught Danny Everett, once, standing outside the door to the front end of the apartment, openmouthed—though he immediately made a wisecrack and ran off. (I like to think he's a fiddle-player somewhere now. It would serve him right.)

Come in. Come in, Danny Everett.

> Here is the room
> Where the music is made.
> Here is the room
> Where violins are played, and light is made
> Of light, and sound falls to the ground like fruit
> Shaken from a full tree.
> . . . .
> Here is the room where violins are played.

The Guadagnini itself is only the usual curved, hollow, varnished box, dark red, with highlights of gold, and start-and-stop stripes of a blacker hue. Its pedigree is recorded in books, its history in our hearts. The line from the top is generally this: Stradivarius, Guarnerius, Guadagnini, but a particular *this* may exceed a particular *that*, and my father's Guadagnini is one of the best, "completely authentic in all its parts," and would equal many a Guarnerius.

It is called "The Ex-Kingman" and was made in Parma in 1769, and its "provenance," as it's called, comprises W. E. Hill and Sons of London, A. Kingman of Montreal, William Lewis and Son of Chicago, and Milton Cherry of Baton Rouge.

Mother didn't get her good violin, a Soliani, until years later. ("What *I* want," she had said, "is a beautiful fiddle with a golden color and a golden tone." And my father, determined, found her one exactly like that.) In those Ithaca days, she was still scrubbing dirty clothes by hand in the bathtub, pushing them up and down the side of a washboard and wringing them dry through double rollers. But both my mother and my father had what it took to be string quartet players—dedication, selflessness, and impeccable technique—and she held her own. If just the two of them were playing, they'd keep a footstool between them to hold their ashtray and cigarettes, Mother's Cokes and my father's coffee cup and saucer. Another reason we went hungry was that our parents sometimes simply forgot to feed us.

It was worth it. My sister and I never doubted that. When our parents put their fiddles away for the night, and we watched our father wrap the Guadagnini in its white satin scarf—reverently, but efficiently—we knew for sure that it was necessary to render not only unto God what was God's and unto Caesar what was Caesar's but also unto Beethoven what was Beethoven's.

I can remember standing at the window in the front room of that "railroad" flat, three flights above the grocery store where with coupons we could still buy rationed oleomargarine, and watching my father turn the corner onto College Avenue after climbing up State Street. It would be snowing furiously—it was always snowing furiously, it seemed, in my childhood in Ithaca, even in spring and summer, even when we were skating on the sidewalk or jumping rope on the playground. It was snowing, and my father was climbing State Street, and his back was bent nearly double to protect the fiddle from the rough winds and cold and wet. The case was black and nubby, nothing special—your ordinary gangster-godfather's violin case. My shy, handsome father wore a hat but he'd have to take it off and mash it between his elbow and side because he needed both hands to carry the fiddle. He carried that fiddle in his arms. It was his life he carried. No, strike that. He would not have thought his life was so precious (and perhaps, I sometimes think sadly, did not know how *infinitely* precious it was to us). It was Beethoven's life he carried in his arms, or the life of music itself, the history and continuance of the art of making music, and I don't believe that he ever held any life so carefully as that one.

Do you think we were jealous—we, the children? But we were *listening*.

Never, I would say, any life so carefully as that one. . . . Some years later, when we'd moved down South again—to Virginia—there was news of a tornado approaching Richmond, approaching, specifically, the Defense General Supply Center, where my mother was working as a buyer. The DGSC (everything governmental has to be known by its initials, so it's lucky for poets that God set Adam down in Eden instead of D.C.) was outside town. My father was teaching downtown. He got in the car and started heading for the place where Mother worked. He had the radio on, listening for news, and then more news did come—a *second* tornado was headed straight for the center of town.

Should he keep going for Mother, or should he turn back and rescue the Guadagnini, which was in his studio in the Fan District? He turned back. As my mother said later, telling the story to everyone she met (because she loved the story), "He did the right thing. After all, I could take care of myself, but that fiddle *needed* him."

Language—let us dare to say, though it may seem at first an inversion—needs writers. The writer doesn't really redeem lost time. That time is gone, is dead; writers can re-make, but they can't resurrect. But writers do redeem something—they redeem all those words that are otherwise lost in no-time. They buy back the language. They give it to the future.

The language is our instrument; words are our voice box, our strings, our soundboard, fingerboard, pegs, bridges, bows, our constructed instrument.

Words are as real as wood. They are as present to sense as the vibrating breath in your lungs, the long glissando of blood in your body. They are as real as anything.

I was wrong when I thought that words were signifiers; I'd have done better to eat those menus whole, gobble them down. Words are not names. They are not tokens. They are what we have. Unlike paper money, they do not depend on Fort Knox for their worth. They are the instruments on which are played all the lives of our fathers, on which are displayed the virtuoso merits of our fathers: Shakespeare, the Russians, the classical poets, the sly philosophers of the East, the best of the Romantics.

Writers have mistaken themselves for creators; they are performers. They make, with their words, a kind of music, it might be said. The composition that they play is time. The composer? We must adhere to our analogy even if it humbles us. "All art," as Pater famously said, "constantly aspires towards the condition of music."

Or one may take the more pragmatic approach of my mother, as exemplified in this story I have often (returning to the scene of the rhyme) written: When I, being then about ten or eleven years old, asked her if she believed in God, she put one of the late Beethoven quartets on the record player and said, in these words that I have played back to myself again and again, changing them only slightly each time, "I don't know about God, but I'm sure there's a Beethoven, and if *he's* in *his* heaven, all's right with *my* world."

Either way, writers are left with their instrument, words, to perform the best they can. In their works, though they try to buy back what they were ever only allowed to borrow—time, and lost life, lost love, the remembrance of things past—writers gain, by inevitable, fantastic, wonderful error, the future. Innumerable futures, that become, for succeeding writers, the exponential base of further futures. This world, and this world, and this world, and all of them as they will be forever, sentence without end.

We are trudging up a hill, and the wind is blowing against us, and it is snowing, and we are carrying, very close to our chests, the words that the language has given us. They are expensive, and we have bought them, if we have bought them at all, on the installment plan. We must not lose them.

We must not lose them. We are obliged to pay for them continually, on time, and we do this gladly, starving for art.

And so, oh, you better believe it, I let myself be as obsessed with this theme as I want: it's a resounding theme—and as I say, when my parents practiced, we listened. I remember that old chestnut about how Beethoven happened to write *Muss es sein? Es muss sein* on the score of the String Quartet in F Major, Opus 135—a heading for the last movement of the last quartet. *Must it be? It must be.* Musicologists like to say he was thinking about whether he was really going to have to come up with his rent that day. Other musicologists who find this joke distasteful say that Beethoven was pondering the great question of free will and determinism.

"The Difficult Resolution. Must it be? It must be. It must be."—
That is the whole notation.

Some say he was referring with amusement to a certain well-to-
do gentleman's having missed another composer's series of concerts,
and the feeling of friends that the gentleman should cough up fifty
florins—the cost of a concert subscription—anyway. "Must it be?"
the gentleman had asked, good-naturedly making fun of himself.

Some see Beethoven making a simple comment on the difficulty
the last movement had given him. "For I could not bring myself to
compose the last movement," Beethoven wrote Moritz Schlesinger,
according to the biography by George R. Marek. "But as your letters
were reminding me of it, in the end I decided to compose it."

And some musicologists read in this rubric an intuition of im-
pending death. Marek rejects this interpretation.

Me, I like to think he was having it all ways at once. Why not?

Because the fishes and loaves won't *even* swell, but the words
multiply. They multiply like crazy, performing miracles of ambiguity,
irony, paradox, and metaphor.

And I could laugh, thinking of words in love with words, of whole
families and tribes and countries of words, words begetting words
begetting words. I don't eat my words—even when somebody says I
should—but redeem the firstborn; I want to save the language from
any god that would devour it.

It's absurd. And it's ironic: a writer could laugh all the way to the
bank, if she had any reason to go to a bank. Where creative artists
are concerned, then, this bank, unvisited, might as well be one of
the Musical Banks of Erewhon, a most peculiar monetary institution,
"[t]he saving feature" of which, wrote Samuel Butler, "was that while
it bore witness to the existence of a kingdom that is not of this world,
it made no attempt to pierce the veil that hides it from human eyes."
Now *that's* funny. Or if I forget to laugh, sometimes, for there are days
when one does forget to laugh, finds nothing ironic, finds everything,
almost everything, absurd, I listen.

I listen to the language.

It reminds us that we are richer than we know.

Why I Don't Keep a Diary

ON POSITIVE CAPABILITY

I USED TO. Stopping over at my grandmother's in Gulfport on my way to the New Mexico Institute of Mining and Technology, I wrote in it, "Now I will have to make myself forget my ambitions. For the next few years, I must concentrate on science." I was seventeen, a sophomore.

According to a note in an earlier diary, one of my "ambitions" was "to write works that will show the world women can think as deeply and feel as passionately as men do." At times, I became mystical about my "mission"—it encompassed a whole complex of ambitions —which I then translated into imagery involving deer, roses, rain, snow, and dead birds. A lot of dead birds. In my succeeding diaries —plural, because I kept misplacing them among my other papers—I wrote about my lack of humility and about how I needed to cultivate a sense of worthlessness. As I felt like a failure in any case—I was now nineteen and had neither discovered a Unified Field Theory nor published a novel nor found a husband (and finding a husband was what, at that time and in that place, nineteen-year-old girls were expected to do in lieu of discovering a Unified Field Theory or publishing a novel)—keeping this diary was a little like beating myself over the head, but then, that was probably the point. The diary as self-flagellation. The diary as hair shirt.

At nineteen, I was living on the top floor of a remodeled carriage house on a campus in Virginia, having failed even to "forget my

ambitions." From the dormer window I could see green grass, a
gravel path. There were climbing roses on the outside brick walls,
and the smell of them filled the room when the windows were open.
It was a plum room. I sat at my desk on sunny days writing in my
diary about the holy deaths of deer and sparrows, about sacrifice,
and so forth.

Graduation rescued me. I went off to study philosophy and soon
was too busy writing papers about Hume and Frege to have any time
for diary-keeping, much less dead birds. What spare time I had, and
some that wasn't so spare, went to poetry and pool—writing poetry
and shooting pool, the latter supplying a needed base in reality, I
should think, to the former. But after a couple of years I found myself
in Europe, where it seemed obligatory to maintain some sort of record
of my impressions. By now, I was skeptical of diaries, so I wrote a
series of letters to my parents which we had agreed, before I left,
to call *Letters from Amsterdam*. My parents fitted them into a folder
with a label on the front saying that. When my parents retired to
England in 1975 and sold the house, and we all went through our
things, deciding what to sell and what to hang on to and what to pitch
out, I came across the *Letters from Amsterdam* and the religious diary
from Framar Dorm, my Booth Tarkington diary and even the diary in
which I had recorded my "ambitions." I packed them up with poems,
stories, notebooks, one-act plays, rough drafts, finished versions, a
History of the World I wrote in ninth grade, and a thousand scraps
of paper, and stored them away in a warehouse on the Petersburg
Turnpike. The stuff's still there.

The critics tell us, and they are not wrong, that modern art traces
the introjection of the artist into the work of art. Now a nearly
total reversal seems to have taken place, and instead of negative
capability, a type of positive capability is the writer's aim, as he
tries to make the reader conscious of the creating mind that animates
each of the characters on his page. I call this "positive" capability
because it requires the *addition* of the writer's self to the already
given of the world, real or imagined.

James Joyce, of course, is the ace practitioner of positive capability, wielding in the novels a style, or styles, so gratuitous that

the reader is forced by the clear absence of any reason for such language to recognize the writer as the only cause of it. What had seemed essential—the work—is nowadays contingent; and what was secondary—the writer—has become the one necessity.

In one sense, then, the diary looks like the mode *par excellence* for the writer in the twentieth century. Perhaps it even is, at least for female writers. Where their diaries aren't frankly labeled, as in Anaïs Nin's case, they may be disguised as novels, or *Letters from Amsterdam*. The autobiographical novel which so many women have written is less fiction than diary not because it is autobiographical but because its structure is the day-to-day, or month-to-month, jotting down of life as lived. There is no imaginative reordering of time. It is diary-time, Wednesday the tenth following Tuesday the ninth. Christmas is just another day.

What I am trying to say is, I think that the disguised diaries of dissatisfied ladies and the elaborate wordgames of self-conscious men are twin phenomena, offspring of the same parent.

Why keep a diary? To answer this, I devise an experiment. For three days, I keep a mini-diary, recording events:

May 5, Fri. Party at L's. Discovered M schoolmate of Sylvia Plath at Smith. Says Plath got Ted his start. Also says Plath was bossy; the girls all hated her. Oh dear. Listened to M, missing X.

May 6, Sat. Hung over. Read newsp. Office at two. Worked while greatly missing X.

May 7, Sun. Saw X.

Plath readers will say May 5 was the important day in this diary; my readers, some of them anyway, will swear May 6 is the day that counts. But for me—let me tell you, the day to remember was the seventh of May.

So the experimental diary-keeper goes at it another way and writes about what she *thought* during those three days:

May 6, Sat. That the passage of time means we are constantly becoming what we aren't. . . . Dialectical anxiety.

That's the sole entry. (I figure thoughts and outward events occur in a ratio of approximately one to three, unless you're Einstein. Even if you are Einstein.)

Predictably, I then discover you may try keeping your diary a third way, recording your *feelings*, but I discover also that if you do, you don't cite an example here for all the world to see; you buy a diary with a small gold lock. (X is grateful.)

That leaves the diary of observations:

> *May 5, Fri.* Party at L's. H overdressed in ankle-length pink print. M's face glows when she talks about Plath. Q without R, wonder why. B sick and had to leave. W's hand on O's thigh in kitchen. X's wife here with her lover. I (not I.) left at eleven.

> *May 6, Sat.* Rain and high winds. From my office window, lake looks cold, is choppy.

> *May 7, Sun.* The shadow of the free-standing clock on the wall behind it. X was here, came in soaked. (It's still raining.) When he said we shouldn't write to each other, his hands shook. I said I agreed. And then he took my address. The travel alarm on top of the footlocker ticked symbolically in the otherwise silent room. We almost laughed. Said farewell, farewell. X gone. Missing X.

Oh, but I don't know why anyone would want to read about unhappiness already lived through. Nostalgia? To remind oneself of what one can survive? . . . There's even less point in putting down the good things, at least while they're happening, since before you can write about a walk in the woods you must sit down at your desk.

So much for my literary lab. The results are in: diaries don't tell things true; diaries lie by *not* lying, by not revising history, facts, to meet the demands of meaning. Art, of course, does something else than simply note good times and bad; it places them in interesting relations to each other, it suggests causes and consequences, it stands, if necessary, time on its head. In my diary, I am merely missing X, but his presence, even his absence, informs my *poem* or *story* the way light informs day.

(Instead of keeping a diary about myself, I will keep one about X.)

∽

I come back to this thought, peer more closely at my parenthesis. Suppose you should do that . . . suppose you should go so deeply into somebody else's head that you might write his diary for him. Under such *other* circumstances, you relinquish your own being in the world. You lose yourself, you become what you aren't. Rather than locating yourself in relation to the world, you—the you that there is —are willing to rest in "uncertainties, Mysteries, doubts, without any irritable reaching after fact & reason," tolerating all contradictions to your own character, melding with that Other. You experience the world by subtracting yourself from it.

Keats's concept of negative capability seems to me, therefore, intimately linked with the act of *significant* creation. It is not simply that one is curious about how the world looks to others, though curiosity is certainly a factor; it is that art, as the very antithesis of diary-keeping, requires a radical overturning of the self, a revolution in the soul, which breaks the connection between time and experience so that the ground wires of both may be rerouted to create light where previously was darkness. To become negatively capable is to escape the self *as it exists in time*.

I play with this a bit, for the fun of it; I imagine God creating the world by withdrawing from it; the farther he retreats, the more "authentically" it exists, all that can be conceived taking substance from the act of self-abnegation which is imagination, until, at the pinprick moment of perfect concentration when even infinity becomes real, God winks, like a light, and extinguishes himself.

Okay. The writer imagines her world most fully and convincingly as she forgets herself. Six days she thinks it into being; on the seventh, she knocks off for a drink.

What about the writer whose intent has been just the opposite, to make *you* one hundred percent aware of *him*? He can never quit, leave off, go away. A continuous buzz emanates from his work, a manic hum. It is as if the voice in the bush never shut up: *I am that I am*, it says—and says, and says again; *believe me*.

Or take, as it were, the lady who won't run the risks of tampering with time; that same reluctance to dislocate the self from the known world is evident here too, the constant reiteration of time as-it-has-been serving the self's chronic need for ontological security. *I am that I am, I was that I was, I will be forever.*

These two, the gamesman and the autobiographical novelist, do not create autonomous worlds for the reader, nor do they even solicit the reader's aid in imagining worlds; they ask the reader to create the *writer*, to sustain in the reading mind unstoppingly an existence which strikes the writer everyelsewhere as tenuous as sunshine in Oregon: the writer's own. It is as if the writer commanded the reader, *Let there be me.*

I don't keep a diary for the same reasons I used to keep one. I want to forget my ambitions, learn humility, write sentences that begin "He said" and "She said," rather than "I said," unless the "I" is someone else, Tennessee Settleworth, say, or Katie Allen. If X doesn't write to me, I may become X and write to myself.

Is this the wisest thing for a writer to do? I don't know, I just know that the opposite course doesn't interest me much. I have already become who I am. Becoming what I'm *not* may be an exercise punctuated by anxiety—cf. the syncopated heartbeat—but at least it isn't dull. As a writer, I can encounter time from a hundred different angles; I stack yesterday, today, and tomorrow any way I like and then deal from the bottom of the deck. Instead of wordgames, I play timegames, and instead of my diary, I write others' diaries. Being a writer means, to me, walking right out of your own head, thinking up the world as you go, so that the greater the distance you can place between your thoughts and yourself, the greater your world.

It means writing the world.

I began this little essay in Wisconsin; now I'm in Virginia, near Sweet Briar. I arrived here yesterday and don't feel at home yet; my room, my studio, my typewriter, the people are all new to me. If I were keeping a diary, I would write in it: Am missing X! From one window I can see the dovecote; out the other, there's a pile of red dirt.

My thoughts are with X, and the distance between them and me seems enormous. I may take the next plane out, any minute now I'll start packing.

I remember that I still have books and papers, and a chair with lion's-paw arms, in the A–1 Handi Mini Storage on the Petersburg

Turnpike, which, come to think of it, is not so far from here. Although I don't yet feel "at home," I might be said, after a fashion, to have come home; the terrifically odd thing is that home has gone elsewhere. I feel as if someone's pulled home out from under my feet, like a rug.

I wonder if my old dorm, north from here, still exists, the carriage house. I remember the diary I kept there.

I'm no longer nineteen. I've published a novel. I've even found a husband—somebody else's, it's true, but a husband all the same. Who knows, a Unified Field Theory could be just around the corner.

My ambitions have altered slightly. Now they include "writing works that will show the world men who think as deeply and feel as passionately as women do."

And as I am doing this, musing on such matters as change and similarity, it occurs to me that once again, even within so small a framework as this essay makes, this essay that is not quite a *History of the World*, time, while appearing to pass, has turned around, as if to begin again. This rebeginning time is nevertheless not identical with the first time around; it is the-way-things-were-but-with-a-difference. It is as if Time were a bird—"time flies"—and it dropped from the sky; but because it was caught by the eye of the imagination, it was only stunned.

DORA

said old
dead things
· · · · · · · ,
wings

of
rough birds
that turn harsh
as words . . .

You could look at time the way Dora did; or you could write about time resurrected, flung into flight. *Wordsayer, you have a choice.*

Why I Am Writing Stories
about a Woman Named Nina

POSITIVE CAPABILITY RECONSIDERED

WHEN I BEGAN WRITING—defiantly determined that someday I would show the world that a woman writer *could* think on a grand scale, *could* think largely and logically—an ability that was then supposed by all to be limited to men—I still assumed that the woman writer's protagonists would have to be male. What happened to women, so the wisdom of our critical tradition went, was simply not significant enough to sustain grand structures, unless, of course, it was a male writer, with his large and logical brain, who was doing the sustaining, writing about a female protagonist.

I grew up in the South, in the fifties. I will tell you how much a child of my generation I was: Some time back I was looking through my high school yearbook. In the section on the activities of the Drama Society, I came across a black-and-white photograph of a backdrop stage design for a play for which I had written the script, about the vocational choices we would soon be making. In this backdrop, there is a river—the river of vocational opportunity, apparently—running past a big-trunked, leafy tree. A boy and a girl are leaning against the tree trunk, one on each side, both fishing with reel and rod in the river. Three fish are swimming up through the water toward the boy's line: One says DOCTOR, one says LAWYER, and one says SCIENTIST. And three fish are swimming to the girl's line, and one says NURSE, one says SECRETARY, and one says TEACHER.

Nurses, secretaries, and schoolteachers—male or female—are to be treasured, of course, but it shocks me now to realize that I wrote this script and that it never occurred to me—or to the school guidance counselor—that the DOCTOR, LAWYER, and SCIENTIST fish might ever be hooked by the girl. (Or rather, we know how girls were expected to hook those particular fish back then.)

Creative writing classes not being available in high school or college, I did most of my writing, if not my playwriting, on the sly. At the University of Virginia, some friends, including Henry Taylor, and I attended our own writing workshop, which we called our Bootleg Poetry Seminar, meeting secretly at night under the fluorescent lights of an empty classroom to critique our poems. Richard Dillard (who publishes as R. H. W. Dillard), while not in the class, was another young writer with whom we swapped work and traded comments.

Henry and Richard, who have remained dear friends, are among the thirty-nine writers included in an anthology called *The Girl in the Black Raincoat*, edited by George Garrett, a splendid and brilliantly dedicated writer of bountiful enthusiasms who, arriving there as a young professor, singlehandedly woke Charlottesville from a deep literary somnolence. This book is a compendium of poems and stories about a girl with long hair who wanted to be a writer and always wore a black raincoat. Though this black raincoat sounds very bohemian, and it stimulated the hormonal imaginations of a good many male writers, my mother had bought it for me on the third floor of Thalhimer's in downtown Richmond. Having a book written about me was fun, and I look back on the surrounding time of it as a mostly marvelous, chrysalid stage bursting with friendship and the energizing excitement of literary discovery—because every one of us managed to make at least one literary discovery a day and couldn't wait to clue another of us in on it—and so the book is a reflection of creative community and a tribute to that time, but it was not quite what I had intended to accomplish in life. I wanted to have a muse, not be one.

Faced with a future in which there were no job opportunities —besides my sixty-dollar-a-week editorial-assistant position at the

Presbyterian Board of Christian Education—I did what young women
of that time did: I escaped into marriage.

My husband, it turned out, was no muse. I quit writing. I taught
algebra and grammar; I learned how to make a white sauce; and
for three years, because I loved him, I took seriously my husband's
views on women, which, inspired by Freud, held that women who
were ambitious were like that because they suffered from penis envy.

It never occurred to me, at the time, that he was envious of my
writing.

After our divorce, and a few years living on my own in New York
City, I began writing again. It was only at this point that I began to
be able to think of myself not just as someone who wanted to be a
writer, or even someone who wrote constantly, but as someone who
was a professional person as well and who would send her work out
to magazines and, when it came back, send it out again.

I quit my current job, sold or gave away everything I owned, and
went back to Richmond and began a novel. I was lucky; it sold the
first time out.

That first novel *did* have a female protagonist, a young medical
student named Tennessee, but she was not myself. Some of her
experiences corresponded with mine—she worked as a governess
in a penthouse that went up in flames—but she wasn't at all like me
emotionally. For one thing, as a medical student, she didn't tend to
faint at the sight of blood.

Keats said that the hallmark of a great writer is "*Negative Capability* . . . when man is capable of being in uncertainties, Mysteries,
doubts, without any irritable reaching after fact & reason." He had in
mind especially Shakespeare's unparalleled ability to submerge his
own personality in that of his characters, being willing *not* to tell the
reader what to think or how to feel, being willing to let the reader, or
playgoer, view the world in all its manifold variety without nudging
him to a particular interpretation of it.

I believe that on the profoundest level, Keats was right. I believe
that a great novel is one that supports contradictory theses, giving
them equal weight, holding together in art the forces that in real
life threaten to fragment our existence. I believe that great art is

not propaganda, even though occasionally great artists thought that propaganda was what they were trying to do.

And so in my first novel and in the next three, I worked hard to keep myself, at least as I perceive myself to be, as far out of the text as possible. Until one day it dawned on me that I might be working even *harder* to do this than most male writers I know. Harder even than Henry, Richard, and George. Negative capability is, after all, an idea that is likely to be particularly attractive to a woman: it confirms everything women have already been taught about how to place others before themselves. We were taught to keep ourselves in the margins of the texts of our own lives—why wouldn't we like the idea of doing the same in our books?

And that was when I thought, All right, Shakespeare and Keats may have been on to something—but maybe they also overlooked something. Maybe, just maybe, they overlooked *positive* capability.

What would positive capability be? It would be first of all the willingness and ability to use one's own experience in the formation of one's characters. I am not talking about autobiography here; I am talking about a kind of risk-taking, an unashamed borrowing of materials from oneself. The risk is in the exposure, of course, but that is not the only place the risk is located. The risk is also in the separation of those materials from oneself. It is in ripping them away from the self and handing them over to *characters*.

What had previously seemed hubris now looked to me like an act of generosity. And a very demanding act of generosity, at that—one requiring a degree of ontological security. If you are going to hand over part of your experience, you'd better feel you are still whole without it.

But another thing positive capability would be is *positive*. It would be a validation of one's own experience and oneself, a testament to the belief in the reality and significance of oneself. And this, of course, was not an easy thing for a woman of my generation to come by, though it is something women writers of my generation hope we have helped women writers of a younger generation to feel entitled to as a part of their literary legacy. For younger women writers do inherit a literary legacy, and that will make a difference—what kind of difference remains to be seen—in the kind of work they produce.

Their legacy will include the characters that some of us have created in our explorations of capability, positive and negative. It will include the characters we created when we wrote ourselves into existence.

And so I, for example, created Nina. Nina has shared some of my experiences, missed others, and had some I haven't had, but her emotions are mine. She is who I would be if I were living her life. And what a glorious thing it is, a sort of freedom, not women's liberation exactly but a writerly liberation, to be able to step onto the page and say to the reader, "Here I am. This is my life, which I hope you will want to be a part of. It is a woman's life."

Following Marilyn Monroe
(Through Nineteenth-Century Russia)

ONE DAY IN JUNIOR HIGH I read in a movie magazine that Marilyn Monroe was reading a book called *War and Peace*. I don't remember whether this was before or after she expressed her desire to play Grushenka in *The Brothers Karamazov*. But both references pointed me in the direction of the Russian novel, and I have never gone anywhere I like better.

Probably kids today aren't naive enough to imitate their elders in everything; the media provide them with stars of their own. When I was growing up, we knew we weren't yet—weren't grown up yet—and therefore we worked like crazy to get hold of and put on all the habits of adulthood, from high heels and mascara to anxiety. One result was that none of us ever set out to become a writer. We set out to earn a living—and wrote late at night, eyes red and nerves jumpy, believing writing was a calling, not a career.

I think today's tack, with writing classes and poetry readings and the confidence that comes from a concentration of effort which society gives its consent and, even, approval to, is better, certainly less lonely. Only it occurs to me, as day begins to dawn, that I can't help missing Marilyn in ways too circuitous even for Norman Mailer to follow, as if, low along the snowy steppes, after three frisky horses a troika skated, inside of which a dreamy, self-serious, eager and exacting young woman was carried away toward her future, and mine.

On Autobiography and Fiction

In January, 1965, I boarded a train from Amsterdam to Moscow. I was so young then, and so shy, that I would spend whole days indoors, because if I went out someone might actually see me, and the shock of that—of being seen—was more than I could regularly deal with. So I cannot explain how I came to be riding on a train, by myself, to a country few Americans had gone to, a place where I would be not only seen but under the diligent surveillance of spies. For there *were* spies, and they followed me everywhere. Especially after I met Imant Kalnin, a young Latvian composer who had come to Moscow to attend rehearsals of his First Symphony, their interest quickened. This may have been prurience, but since Imant was a declared anti-Communist, it was also, from their point of view, a professional duty. And they were smart to be dutiful: neither Imant nor I could tolerate authoritarianism in any form. No artist can. Art requires of the artist a belief in his or her own view of the world regardless of how many orthodoxies that view may diverge from.

In 1965, it was not possible for Imant and me to get married. In 1975, we decided to try again. I went back to Latvia. This time the spies turned out in full force—part of the game is to let you know that you are being spied on—and Imant was threatened by the Central Committee, and attempts were made to frighten me, and, in short, we learned that the extent to which the Soviet government sought to intimidate us was an accurate measure of the extent to which the government was afraid of *us*. We were a problem because we dared to be ourselves, and just as authoritarianism hates true art, bureaucracy

40

cannot abide individualism. Soon my visa expired. "You must say our story to the world," Imant told me. "Say them what such rulers are doing."

Just a few months earlier, I had written a short story titled "Where the Winged Horses Take Off into the Wild Blue Yonder From," about "Pēteris" and "Kate." Pēteris is in a situation very similar to Imant's, but he is scarred by a deep despair that spurs him to extravagant behavior. Kate is in a situation very similar to the one I was in, but she is not at all shy, and she has probably never had a panic attack. Characters so different from Imant and me couldn't make the same choices Imant and I made, and so the fictional story develops differently from the way our lives developed. In fact, it quite quickly develops itself all the way out of personal history into the imagination, where all kinds of made-up events and people and objects enter the scene. When Imant said, "You must say our story," I knew that he did not mean for me to write fiction; he meant for me to write *our* story, not Pēteris and Kate's.

So I settled in and began to write. First of all, I wrote down everything I could remember, and I also wrote down everything that transpired as I made the rounds among embassies and consulates and state departments and home offices, as I beseeched congresspersons and Latvian emigrés and Soviet dissidents, and as Imant and I, our correspondence interfered with by censors, hit on methods of smuggling messages to each other. I wanted to keep track of every detail; I also wanted to understand how the details added up, and that meant long days and nights of thinking about concepts like justice and love and freedom. I had done graduate work in philosophy, but I didn't want to parrot received ideas. There came a day when I said to myself—not out loud—"Okay, Kelly, when you shut this door, Plato and Aristotle are going to be *outside*, in the hallway. They can't kibitz, and they can't help. You are going to think these things through for yourself, logically, even if the terms in which you think about them are metaphorical." Of course, I didn't know that it would take fifteen years to think through everything.

It took me fifteen years to write the book because, as I say, I had a lot of thinking to do. Also, I had to decide what to leave in and what to take out; this is the chief technical problem a writer of autobiography faces. I wrote the book from beginning to end—and in the beginning it was over six hundred manuscript pages—at least once every eighteen months and sometimes once a year. But where there needed to be an ending, there was only a void, like censorship, a point where, because there was nothing more that Imant and I could do, because we could no longer even get letters back and forth, the narrative thinned to nothingness. I couldn't finish the book until life supplied the ending.

In May, 1988, long after Imant and I had realized we had to quit our attempt to battle the Central Committee, and get on with our lives, and he had married someone else, years after either of us had gotten a letter from the other, my telephone rang to tell me that Imant was in New York having been given a visa at the last minute in connection with the premiere of his Fifth Symphony. Flying to see him, I relived those years of sadness and separation, but when we met, in the airport, it was as if one of us had had to go away on business for a weekend and now we could pick up our normal routine.

Except that we couldn't.

I told him that I had tried to "tell our story" but that I didn't think it would ever be published. After all, it was a story with an unhappy ending—though now it could *have* an ending, if he still wanted me to write it. "You must say it, please," he said again. "Whether it is published or not."

I told him that in the current version his name was "Juri." I had given phony names to all our Latvian friends. Should a Soviet authority ever read the book, he would certainly know who was who, but fake names would prevent the book's being used as any kind of evidence. Though *glasnost* was much in vogue that year, I knew that there was more of it in some parts of the Soviet Union than in others. Things could still be scary in Latvia.

Imant nodded, agreeing that I should not use our friends' real names. But he objected to the name I had picked for him. "Is too Russian," he said. (Spelled with a *J*, "Juri" is a perfectly good Latvian name, but Imant was sensitive on this point.) "Besides," he said, "you must say who I am. Otherwise, would not be honest."

I reminded him that he had a wife as well as the KGB to think of.

"Yes, yes," he said, acknowledging potential consequences and dismissing them at the same time. "Kelly, you must use my name, please. Is right."

And so I did. The book was published in 1991. I sent an inscribed copy to Imant, via courier, and one night—long after I'd concluded he had not gotten it—he telephoned me from Riga to say he had read it—this book about a regime that had dominated our lives but now had crumbled like anything stale, desiccated. Perhaps there were too many emotions being felt during that call to specify them all—they included his pleasure with the book, my relief that it met with his approval, our sense of loss, and a shared jubilation sharply edged by historical awareness.

We could write to each other now, but we don't; some things belong to the past, although I would be a liar if I did not admit that I have caught myself, from time to time, daydreaming about the future that did not happen. A future that, ironically, would now be possible—if we were still young, or still shy and in need of validation by each other, or still willing to give up everything in order to remake the world in the shape of an artistic idea.

Still, I sometimes think, that future *did* happen, and keeps on happening, over and over again, in the pages of the book. In the book, an artistic idea *does* reshape the world. A difficult, cold world is charged with passion and beauty and a belief in the necessity of freedom that cause it to shine, because when anything is charged with meaning it shines like a beacon, it becomes a guiding light.

This is what an autobiographer tries to do. It is what I am trying to do, now, in a nonfiction narrative that is in part about my family, a work in which I have not yet sorted out the issues of names and what to leave in and what to take out and whether to show the book to people who are in it. I have only recently decided to use my own name rather than a pseudonym. (It won't be too much longer before fifteen years will have passed since I began *this* book.)

A fiction writer and a poet, as well, want to light up the world with meaning, and some autobiographers stress the similarities of strategy that exist among nonfiction, fiction, and poetry. When I write in any form I am very conscious of how what I am doing is unlike what I do in the other forms; variation is what makes it interesting to me to work in several forms. Thus it is that when I write fiction, I invent all sorts of things, but when I write autobiography, I try to give back to the reader the past, just as it was. And as it will continue to be, for as long as the book is read, no matter how many governments rise up and fall down. Surely, this *is* a happy ending, this restoration of what had been lost.

Revolution and History

A TOPOLOGY

IN TIME, SOME PATTERN APPEARS, some repetition or return threads its way through the broad loom of a life so that even what had once seemed revolution reveals itself as echo, consequence, history. This is the way things are. I am sure there is a mathematical explanation.

And if there is such an explanation, it must be, obviously, topological, a codification of the patterned tapestry that we weave, wittingly or not. At least *I* was unwitting, a young girl from Virginia taking the train by herself to Moscow in January, 1965. Khrushchev had been booted out; there was a troika temporarily in power. There were not many Americans around. I'd read Marx, some Lenin, but nothing in those writers intrigued me. Tolstoy and Dostoevsky, Chekhov and Pushkin, Gogol and Turgenev, Akhmatova and Pasternak were my Russia. Even, in those early days, Mayakovsky. Even Gorky. I remember looking out the window and thinking that I had found something I had, for a very long time, been looking for. I remember feeling suddenly expansive, though I was certainly far too shy to let anyone know how I felt. I looked out the window at that Russian winter, the bright whiteness through which that black train threaded itself, and it seemed to me that I saw in it the promise of a pure, intellectual passion.

I didn't know that ten years later I'd be returning to the Soviet Union with the intention of marrying someone I'd met there (I discovered that an impure passion was also to be cherished). Nor did

45

I know that fifteen years *later*, a full quarter-century after my first visit, I'd return again—unmarried—as a guest of the Literary Fund of the Russian Federation of Writers. The Federation was founded in 1859 by, among others, Tolstoy and Turgenev; I went with three other writers, the first group of writers from the United States to be officially invited and received by the Federation.

It was clear almost immediately even to Americans who were not Kremlinologists of Russian literary politics that some members of the Federation were nationalist and conservative to an appalling degree. Some of them held ideas that could also be located in the minds of Pat Buchanan and Jesse Helms. Should we have refused to meet with them? But, we felt, not just one but *every* Berlin Wall and—though it had still only been parted a bit, by *glasnost*—every Iron Curtain must be torn down—here, at home, everywhere. This is why writers sit on panels and sit through official banquets and sit and talk and sit and listen: to tear down the mind's Berlin Walls and Iron Curtains.

My colleagues—poet, critic, and translator Edwin Honig; essayist, and director of the Virginia Center for the Creative Arts, William Smart; and novelist Candace Denning—and I arrived in Moscow on Aeroflot in August, 1990. We were met at the airport by Valery Dolgov, acting director of the Literary Fund, and two young women translators. The translators presented Candace and me with armfuls of roses. Mine were yellow, the color, I thought, having recently reread Pasternak, of "a candle, burning."

I'd brought along my paperback copy of *Fifty Poems*, translated by Pasternak's sister, Lydia Pasternak Slater, the glued binding cracked with age, pages loose and held together by a rubber band. So many years ago, I had highlighted certain lines in this book, including the admonition to "be alive—this only matters— / Alive and burning to the end." Well, I'd been young. And perhaps I still agreed with what that said, if you got right down to it.

We spent our first few days at Peredelkino, the writers' house near the Pasternak estate. We would then go to Leningrad and during our stay there would visit the writers' house in nearby Komarovo. We would spend the latter half of the month in Yalta, at the Chekhov Writers' House—a sojourn long enough to do some writing in. All along the way, we would meet with Russian writers, officially and unofficially.

It is a strange feeling, when you have been rejected, to find yourself not merely accepted but welcomed. On my first visit to Russia, I had been followed by KGB agents in a white Volga. On my second visit, my then-fiancé had been warned that if he did not stop seeing me there would be unfortunate developments; our liaisons were photographed, taped, transcribed. Now I looked around me— perhaps as I sat on one of the benches of dark green wooden slats in the park at Peredelkino, amid birches and lime trees—and realized, with a start, that if it had not been for Brezhnev I might have been there all along. I might have spent a month precisely there, there in Peredelkino, every year for the previous fifteen years, just like any number of other writers in the USSR. Everywhere I turned, I saw the past that might have been—except a past that might have been is no past at all, is not even a future. There were days when I felt I was living in the subjunctive, a mood difficult to translate.

I didn't really try to translate it to my companions; we were having our own experiences, here in the present, and the fact that my experience of the present was cast against this odd backdrop of a past that had never quite happened seemed to me something it would be bad manners, almost, to mention, or to mention very often. Things happen in Russia—they simply do, to whoever happens to go there—and I didn't want to get in the way of others' experiences. When, for example, we were overcharged at a restaurant in Leningrad and our two translators, challenging the check, were accused of being prostitutes and threatened with the "militia" if they did not disappear, I recognized in myself a sense of déjà vu. Not that I had lived this exact event before, but I had lived something like it—this transaction in which threats were of the "militia," in which bribes were the equivalent of tips, in which women were routinely accused of being prostitutes. In *The Exiled Heart*, I recounted the time I'd been mistaken for a Russian demimondaine in 1975:

> We were trying to get into the Luna Restaurant. The restaurants in the
> Soviet Union don't have enough food to feed everybody who would like to
> eat in them, so getting in becomes a business of who-you-know and who-
> you-bribe; the Russians call it having *blat*, connections. Imant had *blat*

here but the woman nevertheless refused to let us in. A man appeared—
I assumed Imant had asked to speak to the manager. The manager was
shaking his head. "Tell him from where you are coming," Imant said
to me. Secretly pleased at having passed for Russian, I said, "I'm from
America." I must have sounded authentic, because we were abruptly
ushered in and given one of the better tables. . . . I kept pestering Imant
about the conversation at the door, wanting to know what the problem
had been. Imant didn't exactly blush, but color rose in his face, and he
began to fiddle with his fork, drawing the tines across the tabletop as if
he were clearing it with a miniature rake. Did they have rakes in Latvia?
Tripping over my own pun, *I* blushed. "What calls what you are wearing
on your legs?" Imant asked. Startled, I said, "Tights."

"Yes, tights. This the problem is, which you are asking about."

I still didn't understand.

"Here there are many Russian whores who wear these black tights for
standing in the cold. At first, they think you are one."

I had passed for Russian, all right—a Russian prostitute. Imant started
to smile in spite of himself, but just then a suspicious-looking man asked
me to dance. He really did look as if he'd emerged from behind a potted
plant and I started to say no, but Imant whispered to me to say nothing.
My would-be dance partner went away. I still don't know if Imant thought
the man was KGB, or if he just didn't want us to lose time while I
explained my nationality to someone else. Or maybe he thought the man
was going to offer me a couple of rubles.

My concern was only for the translators; I knew we Americans
had nothing to worry about, given the official auspices we were there
under. But the translators, who had only been trying to keep us
from being overcharged, might have been in serious trouble had not
Bill Smart stood his ground so firmly, refusing to allow them to be
dismissed. Later, after it was all over, the two young women knocked
on my door. "We'd like to go to the hotel bar," they said, "and have
a beer, but we are afraid to go alone." I went with them to the
bar and bought one a beer and one a Coke, and I listened to the
stories of their early marriages—because almost every Russian has
an early marriage that is soon over—and I told them about how I had
almost gotten married, myself, to someone in Latvia, and then they
asked for another beer, and another Coke, and they said, "We were

shaking when we returned to the hotel. If not for Bill, we would have been beaten, yes, and worse." They said that the Mafia were not so numerous in Moscow. But one of them laughed and said, "Now you see that Russians will fight for principles."

That is a proposition that an American might assent to admiringly and be, at the same time, exasperated by. Russians *have* fought for principles—even if not always for the principles I would choose. Russians seem not to share that easy talent for pragmatism that is almost a definition of American history, so that, if American history is a record of compromise, Russian history bespeaks a constant spiritual war waged between idealism and corruption. And God knows, it's a war with uncountable casualties.

For this reason, I couldn't share my companions' enthusiasm for the faces of the old people in Russia. It is true, I think, that in Russia we all four felt liberated, as it were, from the American obsessions with youth and beauty, from the American inclination to equate celebrity with reputation—and that was a freedom to rejoice in, if only for a month, because it reminded us that there *are* cultures whose sense of time, reaching beyond the fifteen minutes that Andy Warhol predicted everyone would eventually be famous for, allows for values predicated on an acknowledgment of antecedents and an awareness of likely consequences. But those picturesque faces so vividly full of identity— When I looked at those faces, I saw, I couldn't help seeing, lives of such pain, such anxiety and sorrow, that it was as if every one was a chapter in Solzhenitsyn's great history, *The Gulag Archipelago*. That was a book, these were lives that had been yoked to a narrative dictated by insanity and greed. The resounding phrase *historical necessity*, it seemed to me, had never had any referent in reality; it was merely an excuse for a certain kind of bad writing, in which the characters are sacrificed to a plot line whose primary purpose is authorial self-justification.

I pumped Edwin for stories about writers. He'd met W. H. Auden at a cocktail party. "Do you like Thoreau?" someone asked Auden.

Auden was drinking a martini and he stared into the glass. "Not my dish of tea," he muttered.

Edwin was our pessimist. He has a noble profile silhouetted against an aura of wild fatalism. *It will go wrong*, he seemed to be saying, about everything, about life, *so why worry about it*. Candace was the cautious one, prepared for every contingency, good or bad. She had brought plastic Baggies and twist-ties, so each Baggie could be apportioned its share of toothpaste, stockings, toys, and distributed in due time. I was the worrier; I worried about whether everything would get done and what the meaning of its getting done or not getting done might be, assuming that it had a meaning, which, I worried, it might not have. (Though frequently mistaken for pessimists, worriers are simply people who have learned to do their hoping in secret; they are not *quite* convinced that things will go wrong and, in fact, they believe that if they can just worry sufficiently about something maybe it won't go wrong.) Bill was our optimist. When Edwin's luggage failed to arrive at the pickup counter, Edwin was ready to abandon all hope and say the hell with it. Bill said, "No, no, it'll show up. Just wait and see." I said I thought it was wonderful how the two of them balanced each other. Bill spread his arms wide. "I balance *all* of you!" he said, beaming.

At the Writers' House in Leningrad, I asked novelist Daniil Granin and poet Aleksandr Kushner if they felt a lack of moral significance in contemporary American fiction and poetry. (A leading question! I admit it.) Granin said yes, that as of about ten years ago he began to feel this. Kushner argued that it was a more difficult question to answer about poetry, because all that is important in a poem is "wonder and beauty" but as Russian poetry is versed it's hard for Russians to judge the wonder and beauty of "vers libre." They both laughed and said I had posed an "indelicate" question, but I rather think they were pleased with a question that helped to take the conversation to a level deeper than chitchat. (And if they were not pleased, I was.) We were seated at a table in a grand old house that was undergoing renovation; there was something poignant about the place—that is, a feeling of elegance and sadness revealed, not displayed, as elegance and sadness are revealed, not displayed, in a piano sonata by Beethoven—though I wasn't sure what it was. "A pure, intellectual passion" might have been felt here, on occasion, by writers in search of such.

At Komarovo, the writers' "colony"—a Soviet writers' colony is only one-third like an American artists' colony; it is one-third more like a resort, and one-third more like a rest home—north of Leningrad, where Anna Akhmatova, whose poems compose a testament to the spirit of Leningrad, is buried, we met with Granin again. The question of the day—actually, the question of almost every day, but especially here, near Leningrad—was, "What do you think of Brodsky?" Indeed, I'd been startled, even a little shocked, because it seemed, to my Calvinist soul, a type of superstition, like beatification (making gods of people! praying to mere mortals!), to find that in an upper room of the Akhmatova house there was a display of Brodsky's work, its various editions and manuscripts. (He doodles; he sketches naked ladies in the margins. Dostoevsky doodled too, but not naked ladies.) I think highly enough of Brodsky, but I was finding it ever harder to put new spins on my answer to the question. Not that every Russian really wanted an answer to this question. As we were leaving the panel—there had been a panel discussion following the lunch with Granin—one of them said to Candace, muttering the name under his breath with the infinite daring of an iconoclast, "Brodsky, Brodsky, Brodsky, Brodsky."

Of course, we did a good deal of sightseeing, including seeing some sights I had already seen. Our sightseeing also took in, however, places writers had lived, and these were sites I had not previously been able to go to: we visited Yasnaya Polyana, Tolstoy's estate near Tula, and the house in Moscow where Tolstoy had wintered, writing "The Kreutzer Sonata" and *The Death of Ivan Ilych*. We were taken through the Pasternak house. In Leningrad we visited the aforementioned Akhmatova museum and the Dostoevsky museum and, in the suburban town of Pushkin, the school Pushkin had attended.

We made a kind of pilgrimage to Chekhov's home in Melikhovo— experiencing a peacefulness in the flower gardens and lazy pond and, in ourselves, a corresponding longing for the inner freedom this sanctuary represented—and another to his villa in Yalta. Strolling along the promenade, the Black Sea a bright blue in the sunlight, I saw the lady with the pet dog! And then another lady with another pet dog! And yet another lady with yet another pet dog! I kept wanting to laugh, for reasons not easily explained.

To be a writer in America is to be marginal. To be a writer in America who is also a woman is to be a kind of doodle in the margins, a naked lady, an amusement. Of course, to be a poet, male or female, is to be naked, and perhaps the margin, in America or anywhere, is the place where nakedness can most interestingly, as well as amusingly, reside. On the edge, outside looking in (and not noticed, thus not exhibitionistic), with room to move around in . . .

Although the sexism of Russian men is well known, and although Russian women writers are less often published, less often antholo- gized than Russian men writers, the recognition paid by all Russians to literature as a serious act benefits all Russian writers, men and women. It even benefited this American writer, as I worked in my room on Managarova Street in Yalta, the door to the small, concrete balcony thrown open, the wide window facing a slope of pines and cypresses. If I stood on the balcony, the Crimean mountains rose on my left, and on my right the Black Sea stretched its blue arms toward Istanbul. There was a mystery here, a sense of something so ancient and essential that one wanted to submit to it. Mist enshrouded the mountains, or rain fell darkly in them, and it seemed that gods must still inhabit those high, secret places, dangerous gods that would tempt and seduce, gods that would promise knowledge and might even grant it—but could this knowledge be borne?

"A perfect day here," said a woman named Tanya, "brings the sea breeze in the morning, and in the afternoon, a wind from the mountains." Morning and afternoon, I wrote by hand in a spiral notebook. "Now the Night," I wrote, entering the title at the top of a new page:

The air loud as an imprecation
And the wind like a fist
In the face, God himself hammering
The rain in like nails,
And who won't hang on,
Hang on for dear life?
Something we've done,
Something we've done wrong,
The grass flattened, and rain
Fleeing into the ditch
By the side of the road.
Now the brief flare of light before nightfall,
Sudden as revelation.
Now the night.

Sometimes at night I would stand on my balcony and look at the lights of the harbor, the cruise ships docked and winking, the lighthouse beacon sweeping the sea. *Here in Yalta*, I kept thinking, *three men divvied up the world with the result that, years later, I was not able to marry the man I loved. I might have had a child*, I kept thinking.

It was better to think about poetry.

One of the writers we met in Yalta was a poet, Nadezhda Kondakova, whose complex excursions into the meaning of language are included in a recent anthology, a pairing of five Soviet Language poets with five United States Language poets, published simultaneously in the United States, the USSR, Sweden, and Finland. She was returning to Moscow ahead of us, and we hoped to meet up with her again there, on the day before we were to fly back to the States. "We'll meet you at noon on the bench on the left side of GUM," Bill Smart said, referring to the huge department store on Red Square. We waved our left hands, trying to make our directions clear to Nadezhda and her college-student son. I wasn't sure we had succeeded. "Do you think they know *left?*" I asked Bill, doubtfully.

"*Left!*" he exclaimed. "Do they know *left!*" He turned back to Nadezhda. "We'll meet you at the *bolshevik* bench," he said. They broke into large smiles.

(And later, when we were discussing with Valery Dolgov the different possibilities for communication, Bill asked if the Russians had party lines. *"Party lines?"* I asked. "Do they have *party lines?"*)

Our whole month in Russia had been a "Language Lesson," if not a Language poem, and on a rainy day I wrote a poem with that title, concluding,

> All day the rain came down,
> And the earth translated it into trees.
>
> Declined this way,
> The sea may be thought of as the objective case
> Of light.

With a sense of playing hooky, I sometimes used my notebook as a repository for notes that were about poetry instead of about Russia. Rhyme, I noted in my notebook, makes contemporary American writers nervous because they are inclined to assume it is a decorative element, something unnecessary, gratuitous, frivolous. And if rhyme is merely decorative, the writer's task is to come up with ever new, surprising rhymes. . . . Decoration becomes so quickly boring. But rhyme is more than ornament, is an instrument of exploration. So long as humankind is mortal, *dies* and *cries* will rhyme meaningfully. The way to make rhyme new, I noted, was not by thinking up clever words but by counterpointing the rhyme with the rhythm. The strategic placement of rhyme with respect to line break, sentence structure, phrasing, stanzaic pattern, meter, that was what made rhyming an interesting thing to do.

Edwin Honig said that he had met Wallace Stevens at Harvard. Stevens's cheeks quivered from his pleasure at being spoken to—he was so imposing a figure that most people shied away from him at these gatherings. "I met an Abe Honig once," Stevens said. Edwin, whose father's name was Abe, asked his father if he had ever met Wallace Stevens. "Name rings a bell," his father said.

∽

Back in Moscow, on the day before our departure, we parked ourselves on the bolshevik bench at GUM, but no Nadezhda appeared.
Perhaps they had not known *left* after all.

To get to the bench, we had walked into the wind down a street,
the wind raw as anything untamed, a brawling sort of wind, cold, a
warning of more to come. The weather had changed; it would soon
be winter, and it was going to be a winter, we heard on all sides, of
hardship. People's voices were edged with fear, a certain sharp note
of panic. They mumbled words like *military coup* and *dictatorship*
and *shortages*, even *famine*. "There is a new ugliness in the streets,"
a woman said. "People are impolite; they are afraid." We clutched
our collars close against our necks; our eyes teared. Then I looked
up from the sidewalk and saw, across the street, the Hotel Metropol.
It was there, in 1965, that I had first met Imant.

We had been waiting, separately, for the coffee shop to open. He
had been wearing black slacks, a black turtleneck, a black leather
jacket. I lit a cigarette—I smoked then—and he said, later, that that
was how he knew I was American, by the way I lit my cigarette.

At the Writers' House in Moscow, the writer Irina Strelkova opened
a package and brought out traditional Russian head scarves for
Candace and me, the flowers bright as sunshine—or "a candle,
burning"—against a black background. Though it was a *babushka*, I
wore mine around my shoulders to dinner that night, our last dinner
at Peredelkino.

And Nadezhda was there, with her son. They had not been able to
get to the noon meeting because, they explained, a friend of theirs
had been twenty hours late arriving in Moscow. There had been a
wildcat railway strike in Georgia. But the friend had come along with
them to Peredelkino, and now the three of them and Valery Dolgov
and the director of Peredelkino and one of our translators joined us
in a final round of toasts. The next day, delivering us to the airport,
leaving us at the point beyond which he could not go, Valery Dolgov
would say, in a language that, clearly, is *not* dead yet, "Comoedia
finita est."

When the plane lifted off, I remembered that I had already written
about what it was like to be in a plane leaving Russia. My story,

"Where the Winged Horses Take Off into the Wild Blue Yonder From," had ended there—with a plane taking off, making the extraordinary journey we all make, day after day, from reality to imagination, as if these are realms that, however independent, distinct as nations, border each other, so that each is the other's horizon. And I think they are. I think that we travel between them always in search of something, some passion that defines us. *Always*, I had written just a few days earlier, *I mean to stay with you, and always, I am leaving you. It is like a song played over and over, to the point of boredom, or tears. But say that the tears are like rain in the countryside, say that even here, alone in Yalta, I remember you, and it is you I am leaving, you I return to, again.* It is like strophe and antistrophe, this turn and return, this way that things become clear.

Letter from Latvia

CHOOSING INDEPENDENCE

THERE ARE THOSE MOMENTS in which you travel back to some time and place you visited earlier. A trick of light, a confluence of sounds on a summer evening. Sometimes I am fooled into thinking that I am back in Latvia, where August nights around a white wrought-iron table on the grass lasted the length of a candle.

For a moment, then, I imagine what life would have been like had Brezhnev's regime not been determined to prevent the marriage of a Latvian citizen and an American woman who intended to live there. Marriage is one of the rights protected by the Final Act of the Helsinki Accords, but the KGB, who devoted many man-hours to confiscating our love letters and recording sweet nothings, evidently cared nothing for marriage. Or for the Helsinki Accords.

Many of those nights we spent, my fiancé and I, in a room whose wood floor was painted blue and whose three large windows were edged with vines as if they were a gift wrapped with a green ribbon. The room had been turned over to us by the daughter of a family with theatrical ties to Bertolt Brecht. Following in the family tradition, she has gone on to establish herself as a stage director. Sometimes she would visit us, bringing another friend or two, and we would all have tea at a wrought-iron table on the other side of the windows, whispering our ideas about art, music, drama, poetry. We kept our voices low because there could be microphones. Already, my fiancé had been threatened by the Central Committee, warned of what might happen to him, his family, his career if he continued to see me. Futilely, we had tried to reassure Soviet authorities that he had no intention of emigrating.

In fact, the man I was going to marry, the composer Imant Kalnin, could not think of leaving his country. For one thing, it was his *country*—a nation whose independence the Soviet Union recognized in the 1920 Treaty of Riga, declaring that the Soviet Union "for eternal times renounces all sovereign rights over the Latvian people and territory." (I could think of living there, because the United Nations charter specified that I could retain my United States citizenship and passport.)

"Eternal times" lasted until 1939, when a secret pact between Hitler and Stalin placed Latvia, Lithuania, and Estonia under Soviet domination.

Though the spirit of *glasnost* had prompted the Kremlin to admit the existence of this secret and illicit protocol, and though the August coup of 1991 resulted in Soviet recognition of Baltic independence, the *New York Times* quoted Mikhail Gorbachev as saying that the entrance of the Baltic republics into the USSR was "the choice made by their peoples." Choice? Was it a choice to vote when, if you did not, you were not permitted to work? Was it a choice to vote when you were escorted to the polls by eight hundred thousand Red Army troops? Was it a choice when, slipping up, the Communist Party announced its candidates as winners in foreign newspapers an entire day *before* the votes had been counted?

That there was *no* choice had been acknowledged all along by the United States and other Western governments, which refused to recognize, legally, the incorporation of the Baltic states into the USSR. Alas, our public policy on this issue for all these years was a tragic contradiction of precisely those democratic principles President Bush avowed he would uphold. How could we not accord full diplomatic recognition to nations whose independence we insisted on? Not to do this was to violate logic—and human lives.

There was a moral fault line here, a crack through which the hidden visage of realpolitik could be glimpsed, beneath the fine-sounding surface of speeches about democracy. But immediately following the August coup, we were in a remarkable position to correct ourselves: not only the Baltic countries, but we the people, too, had been given a second chance.

We the people—and they the people, for many Russians and other Soviet citizens, disagreeing with Gorbachev, believed the Baltic nations were legally independent and quickly voted to acknowledge the fact—had been given a chance to accord full diplomatic recognition to these small countries without running any risk of "destabilizing" the world situation. Could we reject this great gift, this gift that was like a view through green-ribboned windows opening onto the past, this gift of an opportunity to stand, peacefully yet firmly—and more wonderfully still, firmly yet peacefully—for *ourselves?* Because to affirm Baltic independence was to reaffirm our own.

Waiting for President Bush to take a stand—after Iceland! after Russia! after Mongolia!—I watched, as did so many others, television. And I watched as a cameraman panned the interior of the KGB headquarters in downtown Riga. Then: a close-up of coffee cups abandoned on a table, and an announcer's voice-over explaining that employees had fled just seconds before. The half-drunk coffee, said the announcer, was still warm. File drawers were open or turned over; some of the employees had taken some of the files with them. I stared at the screen, knowing that somewhere in that building would still be the file the authorities had kept on Imant and me. It was a file that had been waved in front of Imant by a KGB colonel during repeated interrogations. It contained photographs, transcripts of telephone calls, the confiscated letters. *Or maybe,* I thought, with a rising sense of triumph, *it's been put through a paper shredder.*

Those were stolen words, stolen pictures; at the same time, it occurred to me that the KGB had never even really succeeded in stealing these memories from our lives, no matter how thick their file was, because, as Imant had asked me to do, I had saved them in my book *The Exiled Heart*, an examination of the nature of meaning. And what was the meaning of those memories? Those August nights on which we talked about art, music, drama, and poetry were, perhaps, our own declaration of independence. Our ideas were independent, we seem to have been saying, our feelings couldn't be dictated, and ideas and feelings would outlast any bureaucracy, because serious art survives.

I believe that, just as I believe that it is an artist's responsibility to do everything possible to safeguard his or her own independence from all who would encroach upon it. So long as an artist has any choice at all, the artist must, as it were, choose independence.

In Latvian folklore, the Castle of Light is a symbol of Latvia's independence. When the Black Knight stole—from the *Bear-Slayer!* —the key to the Castle of Light, the castle sank into the Daugava, darkened and drowned. The Bear-Slayer continued to contend with the Black Knight, for one day he would emerge from the river, key in hand, and the Castle of Light would be returned to its foundation. This day seems now to have dawned—but the United States was not among the first to cheer its early (or say, late, but better late than never) light. In this instance at least, countries around the world revealed themselves as caring more for the principles of democracy than the United States did. We let Gorbachev make the choice for us, privileging an old-boy network above principle. Did we simply not have the courage of our convictions?

Did we simply not have any convictions?

A Candle, Burning

On August 3, 1990, William Smart, Edwin Honig, Candace Denning, and I were welcomed at a reception in Moscow hosted by the Literary Fund of the Russian Federation. Founded in 1859, the Lit Fund was now independent of the Soviet Writers' Union, though many Russian writers belonged to both the Lit Fund (or "Litfond," as it is known there) and the Writers' Union.

The day before, Valery Dolgov, acting director of the Lit Fund, who first proposed this program of exchange between U.S. artists' colonies and Lit Fund "writers' houses," had met us at the airport and whisked us off to Peredelkino, the writers' house outside Moscow near the Pasternak estate. In 1932 Max Hayward, in his "Life into Art: Pasternak and Ivinskaya," referred to the "dachas with generous allotments of surrounding land" that were reserved for writers in "the particularly agreeable country district of Peredelkino." Settling into my room, I fished from my suitcase the paperback of Pasternak's poetry that I'd bought—and carefully highlighted and underlined verses in—almost a quarter of a century earlier. "A candle on the table shone," ran the famous refrain from his love poem "Winter Night," "[a] candle, burning." In my room, there was only an ugly, orange gooseneck lamp, but when I sat at my desk, and the lamplight fell on my spiral notebook—in which I had immediately begun drafting a poem about (amazingly!) a Russian writers' colony—I felt a literary kinship that was like a reunion, which is to say, a return to a part of myself. As I have written in *The Exiled Heart*, I had once planned to live in the Soviet Union as a United States citizen.

I had met a man I wanted to marry, a Latvian, and the future that we might have had, if the Cold War had not prevented it, seemed to me to be almost present, which is to say, almost *past*. I felt a certain sadness, remembering what might have been, but also a healing sense of having recovered some part of myself that had been lost so many years earlier.

We quickly learned that a "reception" in Russia—I do mean the Russian Republic, mostly, as that was where we mostly stayed—is really a sequence of toasts, some of them *pro forma*, such as the toast "to beautiful women," and others springing spontaneously from the experience. It was like a dance, this *pas de*, say, *dix* of compliments. If each of us Americans made some self-discovery during this month, mine was that I have a little-used talent for toasting. Before the month was out, I would toast, among other things, the natural beauty of Russia, Socrates' claim to be "a citizen of the world," and the poetry we made clinking our vodka glasses, the clinking a kind of metrical music or rhyme. I joked that I had found a new literary genre.

And Bill Smart joked, when so much toasting led to one writer's returning to the table with his fly open, "This must be *glasnost*."

The mood in Russia, at least among the writers we met, was a palimpsest of high spirits and high anxiety, jokes that revealed hope and jokes that revealed despair, a kind of book that, though now uncensored, was aware of itself being written over an erased history. Again and again, making the requisite pilgrimage to Yasnaya Polyana or touring Chekhov's house and schoolhouse in Melikhovo —or gazing, as I did, at manuscripts by Akhmatova and Dostoevsky as if by looking at them hard enough I could read those Russian words—we realized that Russia's literary culture was not a branch of the entertainment industry, as publishing so often is in the United States, but a matter of life and death. Indeed, one of the writers we were to meet in Yalta told us that he had had his "back broken" by the "Uzbekistani Mafia" after the publication of one of his books.

I had been to the Soviet Union, including Russia, twice before, in 1965 and again in 1975. I knew what it was like to be followed by the KGB, and I knew how frightened, with good reason, many people had been of talking—even about anything—with an American. How different things were now! Everyone spoke openly. No one hesitated to express an opinion about literature, or politics, or history. Everyone wanted to hear *our* opinions. "And what do you think of Brodsky?" asked one of our translators, mimicking what we quickly learned was a stock question at panels. "And what do you think of Nabokov?"

We learned that although Russians read American writers—Faulkner and Steinbeck; Mark Twain and J. D. Salinger; today's best-sellers; the "realists" who had been acceptable to "socialists" —their knowledge of the more serious of our contemporary authors is as limited as ours is of theirs. "And what do you think of Grace Paley?" I asked. "Cynthia Ozick? Eudora Welty?" Russians are eager to read these writers and others. "Send books," they directed us.

The writers' houses in the USSR are not precisely analogous to U.S. artists' colonies. For one thing, the houses are often used as rest homes or resorts, though I discovered, strolling around the parklike grounds after breakfast or in the evening, there was at least one room at Peredelkino from which the click of typewriter keys issued day after day—a sound I found even more reassuring than the clinking of glasses. In that room, I knew, a gooseneck lamp shone.

At the writers' house in Komarovo, outside Leningrad, the novelist Daniil Granin—whom we had previously met at the Leningrad branch of the Lit Fund, with the poet Aleksandr Kushner, whose collection *Apollo in Snow* has since been published in English by Farrar, Straus and Giroux—joined us for another reception, which is to say, more toasts involving vodka, Armenian brandy, and Soviet "champagne."

Granin's manner is direct and dominant. He gives the impression of being little interested in small talk. But he has a *dacha* in Komarovo, and perhaps, after a day of swimming and writing, it was not too great an interruption to walk over to the writers' house for dinner. He disappeared when it was over, however, skipping the panel upstairs. He was not the only one who wanted to disappear: Russian and American writers alike were initially skeptical of the value of such exchanges. On the way up, a woman of eighty who was still strikingly beautiful, with the carriage only a dancer ever manages—she had been a ballerina and now wrote about dance—

smiled and said to Edwin Honig, in English, "This is going to be very boring."

"What can we do to make it all right?" he asked.

"We can run away," she said.

I believe he was tempted. But when we were all seated in a circle, and had introduced ourselves to one another, conversation grew lively. The Russians wanted to know how our publishing industry works—they were experiencing a paper shortage, and they also expected price increases, as governmental controls were lessened, that would mean dealing with problems similar to those Western writers and publishers face. At a panel in Peredelkino, the writer Yakov Abramovich Kozlovsky had described a "small edition of poetry" as "50,000 copies." This, we explained sadly, was "not the situation with poetry in the United States." We, meanwhile, were trying hard, as we had been since our arrival, to make sense of the numerous factions within the Russian literary world. There were those Russian writers who saw in the decline of the Soviet Union an opportunity for the strengthening of Russian values as traditionally defined, and there were those who saw an opportunity to discard that tradition. We felt it was our duty to be alert to the subtexts of rhetorical statements. It may be precisely this morally mandated task of reading between the lines, as it were, that made our exchange more than an exercise in literary tourism, for both nationalities. Russians or Americans, we had become, for one another, texts, layered and enlightening. By the end of the panel discussion, Russians and Americans alike were sorry to say good-bye. It meant closing a book, or at least a chapter.

After our stays in Peredelkino and Leningrad, we took the train from Moscow to Simferopol, where we were met and driven to the Chekhov Writers' House in Yalta. Situated on the Black Sea, cradled by the mysterious Crimean mountains as if by history itself, Yalta is pure honky-tonk. Vendors and tourists jam the promenade; quick-sketch artists sell charcoal portraits. Here we had almost two weeks to get to know writers, and to write. Our single rooms were about the size of the dormitory-style rooms at the Virginia Center for the Creative Arts, but each contained a small refrigerator and a large TV, and each had a balcony. To my right I could view the Black

Sea; to my left, those astonishing mountains that were surely still inhabited by gods; directly below, unplanted dirt and bits of rusting metal, where construction was still going on.

"The Stalinist period," stated one of the writers at the panel discussion held here, "prevented the natural development of our literature." All of the writers were eager to move away from the artistic legacy (one might say *illegacy*) of the Stalinist period and pursue "the natural development" of their literature. For fiction writers, this seemed to mean a return to novels and stories about personal life, domestic life, love. There seemed to me to be a particular interest in the psychological life of women.

As for the psychological life of one woman— I had been *persona non grata*, for committing the odd crime of falling in love with a Latvian. Now I was *grata*, and it gratified me no end. Sitting on a bench in a churchyard in Yalta, writing in my journal, I was, twenty-five years after my first visit to the Soviet Union, if not quite Chekhov's "The Woman with a Dog," as it's sometimes rendered, at least "The Woman with a Log."

The next month, four Soviet writers arrived in the United States, completing the first of what is hoped will be a series of exchanges conducted through the channel of the Literary Fund. Toasts are not, obviously, a very profound literary genre, but they *are* a little like poems, formalizing deep feeling. Or they may be more like first lines to poems, poems that will be written in rooms around the world, after visits like this one, rooms in which there will be *a candle, burning*.

Poetic Forms as Cartography

POETIC FORMS, ESTABLISHED OR NONCE, are like maps of places no one's ever been. They lead the writer into uncharted territory; they show the writer where to go, even though they cannot know the way. This paradox is what keeps poetic form eternally interesting. If the writer knew in advance what she would find on her journey through the poem, she would not bother to make it. But she doesn't know; she never knows; she knows only that the form is there like a flashlight or map and that she will see what the form reveals and go where the form takes her. She knows, too, that the form *will* take her somewhere, *will* show her a place never before seen or seen so clearly.

I began writing in traditional forms after I had found, in my opinion anyway, my own voice. I was sitting in on a class taught by that exemplary gentleman Allen Tate. He was fastidious in his personal habits and fastidious about poetic forms too, a stickler for the rules: no rhyming a plural with a singular; no shifting of stress for the sake of scansion, and on and on. My first poems in form seemed to me to be a regression; I felt I had learned to walk, even run, and now could barely crawl, tripping over my painfully counted metrical feet as I toddled and lurched through sonnets and villanelles.

But of course, within a couple of years I could see that encountering Allen Tate was one of the truly lucky events of my literary life. I was working in forms all during the time when most young writers were not. It was certainly not all that I was doing in my writing, but it was one of the things I was doing—working in forms.

I find now that I like to use strong rhymes. I like monosyllabic rhymes. I like using the ordinary rhymes others may tend to avoid. These rhymes suit me; so, for that matter, do quatrains. I am very fond of quatrains and blank verse. I like simple words or perhaps I should say *accurate* words, which, if not always, often, it seems to me, turn out to be simple words. I like a complexity that grows out of thought and feeling and imagery and is not embossed on language baroquely.

There is too much showmanship around, too much that is not an honest attempt to make that journey into the poem that is also a journey into the self. (And thereby out of the self.)

But to make that journey—that is a great thing to do, it really is. It is something to live your life for.

A Note about Allen Tate

I took Literary Criticism with Allen Tate. My mind was not on the subject, because—I liked to think—I preferred the abstractions of philosophy and the music of poetry to the explication of the obvious. Literary criticism seemed to me to be mostly paraphrase. But I have since learned to love writing about writing, and perhaps the real reason I was distracted, that bright autumn semester so long ago, was that I had fallen in love. I was going to be married over the Christmas break.

Mr. Tate—we called him "Mr." Tate, not "Dr." or "Professor," and never in our wildest dreams "Allen"—began each class by reading the roll. *Present*, I would say, staring out the window and thinking about licenses, announcements, what dress to wear. *Here*. I wasn't, really.

While he went down the list of last names, Mr. Tate played with his cigarette lighter. It was, I'm sure, a gold lighter. It *looked* gold, and I doubt that Mr. Tate would ever have been happy with something that looked gold but was not gold. He flipped the lid open. Twirled, with his thumb, the little wheel that ignited the wick. The lighter flared. He snapped the lid shut. Sometimes he snapped the lid shut with the thumb of the same hand with which he was holding the lighter; sometimes he gently palmed the lid shut with his other hand.

Oddly, I can't remember whether he smoked in class. It's likely that he did; I think that teachers probably were allowed to smoke in class in those days. But in those days everyone I knew smoked. But not everyone I knew—in fact, no one else I knew—had a gold cigarette lighter. It was the lighter, not the smoking, that was interesting. The lighter, and that Mr. Tate played with it nervously all through class.

He was slender, shortish, with a formal bearing. His manners were of a kind seldom encountered today: the enactment of established rituals of courtesy and consideration. To shake his hand was to participate in a small ceremony. To pass him in the hallway and say hi was to play a minor but, one understood, important part in a well-known drama. (And never a melodrama.)

Maybe there were melodramas in his life. I wouldn't know, because I didn't know him outside of class. He was not the kind of teacher a shy student got to know outside the classroom. Maybe *he* was shy. He certainly did fiddle nervously with that cigarette lighter.

He addressed us with a title, too. We were "Mr." or "Miss." (I have to interrupt myself here to say that although "Ms." had, according to the Oxford English Dictionary, been invented, it had not yet arrived in North Carolina, so he can hardly be faulted for not using it.)

Jonathan Silver and I were married at my parents' house in front of a picture window while the worst blizzard in Richmond's history whited out the view. Guests gazed forlornly at their cars being buried under drifts of snow. Jonathan's mother and father had refused to attend; the mood was solemn, more suited to political and religious history than to romance. There was a sense that we were all engaged in a subversive activity, but against our will, as if we were also surprised, and unsettled, to discover ourselves engaging in anything subversive. People wanted to be in their own homes, not facing the prospect of digging out, putting on snow chains, driving down unplowed roads. As soon as the minister pronounced us husband and wife, coats were grabbed, and people stood in the foyer, sweating in swathes of scarves, waiting only for Jonathan and me to leave first. We had borrowed my father's car. As we turned the corner, I looked back to see the party, which had never quite begun, breaking up. The picture window framed the scene, and it was like something by Hopper, beautiful and sad.

There were two weeks remaining in the semester after the holidays. The first day I returned to Literary Criticism, Mr. Tate, as usual, called the roll, but he did not read my name among the *C*'s. He read most of the roll without stopping. When he reached the *S*'s, he stopped to flick his gold lighter open. Then he called, "Mrs. Silver."

Here, I answered. *Present.*

He flicked his lighter shut and finished the roll call.

That was all. But I knew that this man—this deeply quiet man —had paid more attention to me than I ever had paid to Literary Criticism. Perhaps contemporary women, who prefer "Ms." to "Mrs." and who keep their own names instead of changing them, won't like this story. But I am a contemporary woman, who has reclaimed her own name, and yet I remember the day Mr. Tate called me by my married name as the day I learned what literary criticism is all about. Literary criticism is about the interlineation of text and interpretation. It is about locating new meaning in the words we have been given. It is about knowing how to call the roll—with respect, that is, and observantly, in a way that recognizes change in the world.

Watersmeet

THINKING ABOUT SOUTHERN POETS

I AM ALONE IN A ROOM ABOVE A PUB in Lorna Doone country. From my window I can see the East Lyn—it crashes past, fast and clear, loud as a chorus. Today I walked along its banks to Watersmeet House and back, a three-mile stroll. For eighteen months I have been sitting in another room in another shire, thinking about something, and I have come here for a few days' rest, to walk and to think about something else. I want to think about poetry.

But not any poetry. I have in mind three poets from back home, from Virginia and North Carolina. It was Harold Bloom's *The Anxiety of Influence* that started me thinking about the three of them together. I was reading this book by Bloom, and I got to feeling that somebody ought to take a look at some recent Southern poetry, because Southern poetry is significantly different from other American poetry in a way which helps to reveal the cultural limitations of Bloom's thesis.

Harold Bloom says that the strong poet's direst need is for priority. The strong poet must be, or imagines he must be, "first": almost by definition, he must be a creator rather than a re-creator, and consequently he has got to find some way to deny the effective existence of poetic precursors. This the poet does by misreading —misprizing—his precursors' poems; his own poetry is his "anxiety of influence," his "melancholy at his lack of priority."

71

I don't want to argue with this. It wouldn't be possible to, anyway. Bloom hasn't constructed an argument: there's no means in his system for distinguishing between true and false propositions, and for that reason, it might better be called a metasystem.

What Bloom has given us in the theory of poetic misprision is a flurry of aphorisms, a snowfall of insightful statements from that great Cloud of *Knowing*, psychoanalysis, and some of these are very exciting indeed, startling, and even useful—for critics. But do poets do what critics reckon poets do? Criticism is reconnaissance after the fact over a fictive terrain; from the front, it all looks different. For one thing, out here the dichotomy between "strong" and "weak" disappears. Ask one question: who is stronger, the man who suffers more or the man who suffers less?—and watch that dichotomy drop out of sight like a hawk over a hill.

The difficulty with Bloom's theory of misprision, at least from the point of view of a Southern poet, is that it perpetuates Nietzsche's misreading of the New Testament. Now: Nietzsche thought, more or less, that Christianity was a slave culture and that salvation lay in the will to power. Without blaming Nietzsche for Fascism (or Soviet Communism), especially since he is more properly read as a philosopher of aesthetics than of politics or religion, I do insist that these ideas are dangerous for *poetry*, seductive, false, and programmatic. And part of what I am saying here is that it may be I think so because I am a *Southern* poet. There are two or three phenomena that inform our understanding of the word *Southern*. Sociologists point to the tradition of Southern storytelling. Then there is the intimacy with defeat which Southerners share. Then there is the Bible Belt.

The three Southern poets I want to talk about are chosen from what Bloom sternly calls my "intra-poetic relationships." They are members, pretty much, of my own poetic "generation"; they are, for want of a better word, siblings.

I'll start with Henry Taylor, because he started with me—literally. We began our professional lives as writers together . . . in a bootleg poetry seminar at the University of Virginia. He was a student in the college; I had just enrolled in the graduate department of philosophy.

Things have changed now, but in those days students wrote their poetry extracurricularly. Metaphors did not go over big in Logical Positivism and Linguistic Analysis. (There weren't even any writing classes until the following year, although we caught glimpses of Faulkner in front of Mincer's Pipe Shop.) A fugitive—but not a Fugitive—from the English faculty very sympathetically took us up, and met with us under the fluorescent lights of an empty classroom in Cabell Hall to criticize and encourage us. There was a third student in our seminar, but he became a medievalist.

Taylor's first gift was for mimicry and parody—an astonishingly quick ear for the characteristic rhythms of other poets, and a devastating sense of the particular exaggerations those rhythms could lend themselves to. This is a young writer's gift, and it propelled Taylor into publication unusually early, but back of it has been a deeper, sweeter and truer talent, the ability to penetrate and render the characteristic rhythms of other *lives*. In his second book, *An Afternoon of Pocket Billiards*, Taylor gives us more than poems; he gives us people, a series of portraits that are, above all, lifelike, as realistic as Roman sculpture, so that, for instance, the old Rhodes scholar, the father and the grandfather, the fat man, the president— each is unmistakably himself, the poet respecting his material at the most profound level, on the purely ontological plane. They are who they are, and they are characters revealed in action. The old Rhodes scholar, again for instance, lecturing to a class that includes the poet, is caught drifting into his own memories of himself as "a man his friends no longer know," an athlete, a prize-winning pole vaulter. He pauses in the middle of his lecture to gaze out the window, and it is as if

> . . . we, who have known him only in that room,
>   are now amazed to see him in the bloom
> of age, his paisley tie and gold stickpin
>
>   flawlessly in place
> as he picks up speed along the cinder runway,
>   rises once more toward the bar, away
> from rooms and lives he filled with ease and grace.

That lift at the end of the poem, the poet vaulting over the conventional resolution, taking the unexpected route to the other side of silence, is precisely what lends Taylor's poems their realism, paradoxical though it may seem. He catches the swerve of things, the way life has of going off on tangents. The straight line is death. Taylor even uses an epigraph about a straight line and how it doesn't exist. It doesn't exist because it is the absence of existence.

So it is this straight line, nonexistent in nature but ever present, like a dotted line cutting across a graph, that centers these poems and makes their sweetness true. There is no sentimentality here, no easy relaxation into extremes, but a careful balancing between points, like a mathematical wave plotted between upper and lower quadrants around an invisible horizontal bisector, a graceful dancing curve. There is oddity, flight, an unclassical escape from the horizontal, but it is movement held classically in place by knowledge of the horizontal. It is a knowledge that can turn acid, as in, for example, "Campaign Promise," or this wicked epigram, "To an Older Poet," which should please Harold Bloom no end—and anyone, who is not an older poet:

> Young for my years, impertinent, perhaps
> a poet and perhaps not—so you said.
> I remind you, in a momentary lapse
> of taste, that when I'm your age you'll be dead.

But more often, Taylor's poetry, weaving words around that same grim line, underwrites the community of life. A sense of Christian community—that is the large and vital compass of these poems.

Henry Taylor was brought up in the Society of Friends—a Quaker. Two beautifully tempered sestinas, bracketing his book, comment explicitly on the meaning of the Friendly Sunday Meeting, and "the old clash // with all that fathered me," a clash which is resolved into "music / free of pageantry or sound" when the poet makes a "Return to the Old Friends."

Previously, in "Goodbye to the Old Friends," the poet had said: "Christ has risen. / With the tongue of a man he speaks to me / and to his Friends: there are no angels here." No angels—but there are animals. This community is not parochially human; Taylor knows it extends in charity to dead Percherons and one-eyed jumpers, toads and turkeys, and his translation of St. Francis's "Canticle of Created Things" is no simple exercise but an exact expression of sympathy. In his masterful title poem about billiards, Taylor, considering the game's "random shifts" on "a green field of order," explains,

> I see, as I move into another rack,
> that all days in this cavern are the same:
> endless struggles to know
> how cold skill and a force like love can flow
> together in my veins, and be at peace.

Cold skill and a force like love. *An Afternoon of Pocket Billiards* is dedicated to "old artificers." The impulse that drove it into being is not a competitive one; it derives from the author's awareness that we are all creations of an Old Artificer.

It is the Easter season, and all over the moors the baby lambs are frolicking. They kick up their heels, skip, scamper and gambol just the way they do in children's cartoons. The smallest ones have fleece as white as the Hoar Oak Water tumbling down to the East Lyn at Watersmeet. Their curly coats look like spray scooped up and frozen on the green fields: flocks of white water. When I leave the open road and go under the sessile oak, the larch and beech, I see buds on the branches. Rain pitches down with a sound like someone throwing tacks on my umbrella. I head back in boots caked with mud.

Taylor is one of the few poets of my generation who take a serious interest in the stanza, or verse paragraph. The meticulous structuring of thought in formal units actually increases the sense of life, of developing character and situation, in his poems, because the reader, progressing from point to point, is able to look back and see where he has been. The poetry of R. H. W. Dillard works in a way almost diametrically opposite.

Dillard's is the darkest vision among these three poets. He writes out of an obsession with original sin, and, like Adam in the Garden, he is driven to *name* . . . to name everything, as if the act of naming itself could bring back that lost world. But he is Adam after the Fall, and the naming is compulsive, tinged with mania, a kind of deliberately erratic brilliance designed to light up each object in the universe separately, to divide rather than unite, and stanzas and ideas seem to slide away into wildly careening fragments; the stanzas are arbitrary, because the one *necessity* in this poet's world is "necessity of blood."

> Adam's fall lies on you
> Like your own arm in the night,
> . . . .
>
> You see it in all things:
> The goat's hot blood
> And randy eye, tail
> Of the lizard, raven's
> Croak, the buzzard's meal,
>
> Erosion, drought,
> The plague, the rain
> That does not wash it clean,
> Tree's knot, bare wood
> That rots and warps,
> The tumor and the wound,
> Necessity of blood.

I am quoting from *News of the Nile*, the second of Dillard's collections, which owes less to pre-Christian attitudes than to a Christian view of pre-Christian, or unredeemed, life.

"The Nile flows north," bearing names—names of rivers, towns, movies, old gods, old friends. It *is* the "Old World: Grammar." The second half of the book is titled, in a marvelously implicative bipartite part titling, "New World: Geography," and the epigraph here, from Cotton Mather, exuberantly promises to "single out some Remarkables, and glorify our God!" The promise is kept—the remarkables include all sorts of definitely strange things, not the least of which is downtown Roanoke—but the book's true and inviolable direction is away from the "good season." Always there is the "fallen fruit / Splitting in the day's heat," and, remembering this, the book in the end veers southward once more, in "Alligator Night":

> The alligators come,
> A symmetry, hungry order,
> The one equation.

Redemption, resurrection is possible—

> And in the ashes, old fire,
> You stir like a stiff bird
> At dawn, stretch out
> And try your hurt, gland's
> Drain, eye's squint, locked knee,
> Burn in the healed nerve.

But what is *not* possible is to forget. The Fall remains, a real and forever-present fact about the past. "The alligator in the park"

> Sleeps in the sun
> Like a painful memory.

Dillard's poetry is dark, but not gloomy, not claustrophobic. Its obsessiveness is honest, not for show. The reader is not at a sideshow, watching a poet cannibalize himself on stage. There *is* show in these poems—wit, frenzy, pop culture and literary allusion, images piled on so thick that the poem occasionally disappears under them, syntax that sneaks off with the meaning like a kid with a comic book. The show entertains the reader, but its graver function is to distract him just long enough to catch him unawares. Then,

> The brain's boil
> Stirred out, the muscles
> Betray, shame, die.

. . . .

You are nightsoil,
Limed down, lungless,
Carbon and crawling earth.

Richard Dillard was in Charlottesville when Taylor and I were there, though he wasn't in our unofficial seminar. He was a graduate student in the English Department, and the three of us, abandoning Academe to luck and No-Doz, devoted one entire fall to poetry and pool (but maybe we were writing pool and shooting—for it seemed to us a matter of life-and-death importance—poetry?). Taylor had a white suit, and a cue stick in a black case. I had a problem. I couldn't see to shoot without glasses, but when I wore them, they slid down my nose and I couldn't see anyway. Taylor became an accomplished pool player; I was forced to give it up when I moved to a city where there wasn't a pool hall a girl could play in; but Dillard played to keep us company and cracked jokes to keep us cheerful, and now I find in his poems a similar playfulness, slightly sad, slightly crazy, an aura of all-night sleeplessness, warding off, until the fatal moment of wakening, the old, bad dream—guilt.

In the evenings I sit in the pub and talk to the locals. Dudley —"Cuddly Dudley"—does weddings for a living: he drives brides to church in his dray. He has a West Country accent I can barely understand. I drink gin but don't feel it in the morning. The air is cold—a fine day for an excursion to Lynmouth. It's where Shelley sat on his stoop, blowing soap bubbles.

Fred Chappell's *River* is the first in a quartet of book-length poems. Where Taylor celebrates goodness, and Dillard, like a mountain preacher, reminds us of our damnation, Chappell belongs among the moralists; he is one who, unflinching, tries to define good and evil—a crucial poetic occupation mostly forsaken in this era of lyric effusion. Chappell has an extraordinary command of technique, and his moral stringencies come in a variety of metrical inventions.

In eleven sections, *River* moves from morning to morning—"deep morning." In a sense, this is an occasional poem, a public statement of the poet's thirty-fifth birthday. The different sections chart the river's, and the poet's, moods, in free verse, blank verse, couplets, terza rima, in narrative, epistle, hymn—a heroic technical flow—and yet the parts of the poem are successfully subordinated to the whole, which is an argument in favor of "preparing to voyage / wherever these midnight waters / stream."

The speaker of this poem has taken on an awesome job, and a little self-congratulation wouldn't be altogether inexcusable—but there is not even a flicker of grandiosity anywhere, no self-consciousness about the size of his role as speaker. With an engagingly modest amusement that would give Descartes cat fits, the poet, nearing his conclusion, says,

> What I know is, no one sleeps apart.
>
> Ever ever
> In unanimous voice we drift,
> Selflessness of energies bright and blind.
> We are each of us. There is no me.
> (I do not mind.)

This is an earned conclusion. It is wrung from a "[m]ind coming apart to water," and "water, like human / history, weeps / itself into being." But history is not time, and, as the poet tells us, "Time's not a river."

> On the bank of Time I saw nothing human,
> No man, no woman,
>
> No animals or plants; only moon
> Upon moon, sterile stone
>
> Climbing the steep hill of void.
> And I was afraid.

Human *history* exists in despair of this barren, rock-strewn reach of time; it predicates itself through the fact of suffering. It is in suffering, in undergoing the presence of other beings, that we establish our own existence. Then, and only then, we can say, "We shall not fear" because "[w]e are moving still." The speaker who began by wryly admitting, "[E]ither I live with doubt / Or get out," in the course of his poem has succeeded in converting doubt into faith; that is, not to doubt is to be dead, but to doubt is, above all, as Thomas told us, to feel, and feeling is an act of courage. The other side of fear is faith.

> Our life is gratefully asleep.
>
> Never never
> Would I wish to wake, except to kiss
> Your dark eyelids febrile with dream.
> Never will I wake your eyes.
> The earth is shoving us to sea, the sea shoulders us
> To another earth.
> So we stand naked and carefree and holding
>
> In the dew-fired earliest morning of the world.

And here we have arrived at the idea that is behind all of the poetry I have been discussing. It is the idea of resurrection. The idea of resurrection, of the old made new, the last made first, the dead quickened—the Good News—is common to these three poets, as, truly, it is to most Southern writing, and though there are as many approaches to it as there are people, not to mention poets, no way is comfortable. Nietzsche was able to accuse Christianity of being the consolation of the weak only by emptying the crucifixion of its content.

A couple of years after I left the University of Virginia, I went to North Carolina, where Fred Chappell was one of my examiners. The essay question he set was, Name three writers who have not influenced you and say why. I remember I chose Shakespeare, Dostoevsky—and Nietzsche. My point was that these are writers who cannot be said to act as influences on us, because, like it or not, they *are* us; without them, we wouldn't be what we are wont to call "modern man." They are part of our cultural DNA. But does their having come before us mean that we are "latecomers" in the tradition of literature—or does it not mean, rather, that the vocabulary we start with is so much the richer? Will the poets who come after us (if there are poets who come after us) occupy a narrowing space, or an expanding space?

Bloom says the strong poet misreads his poetic precursors in order to clear imaginative space for himself, but I suggest that only unimaginative poets do this. Imaginative space is infinite. A woman, for example, knows that there is exactly one difference between rape and lovemaking: her glad consent. It is one difference, but it is all the difference in the world.

In his commentary on John Hollander's poem "The Head of the Bed," Bloom wrote, "All men are belated in their stance towards all women. All Kabbalists and Gnostics are latecomers in their stance towards divinity." If this kind of intuitive generalization is allowable, perhaps it is not unreasonable to say that the Southern poet, inescapably cognizant of his receptive femaleness in relation to the Spirit, sees himself as a new-comer, one who knows that influx is the precondition for creation, and who knows too that the creation of life is always the creation of death. There is no way to draw a dichotomy here—the two are inseparably joined. Nietzsche wrote bravely about the strong man carrying the child on his shoulders, but every mother knows that she gives birth to a Siamese twin. That doesn't make the burden insupportable.

It is all—or a lot of it is—in the point of view. You lose your life but you save it, and if the world can't sustain this contradiction, it can't sustain itself. According to St. John, Jesus said, "Therefore doth my Father love me, because I lay down my life, that I might take it again. No man taketh it from me, but I lay it down of myself. I have power to lay it down, and I have power to take it again." This is *the merit of the son.*

The Southern poet, then, who grows up even latterly with the Good News as part of his daily bread, and who is maybe more than some guiltily aware of the need for it, is likely, looking at *the merits of his poetic fathers*, to feel not that anxiety which has been wished on him but an expansive exhilaration, a sense of the terrific possibilities of—not of "misreading." Of translation. "In the beginning was the Word." And in the end also.

Tomorrow I take a taxi to Lynton, a bus to Taunton, and a train to Reading. Today it is snowing—huge soppy flakes melting halfway down to earth. It will stop in a second, and then the sun will come out and it will be, for a few moments, summer. In England the seasons change hourly. I don't mind. I can climb a hill and gaze out and downward past yellow-flowering gorse and a tangle of green twigs into dark winter—but I am fond enough of dark winter. At the bottom, a little farther on, that's where the waters meet, and I'll buy a cup of coffee from the National Trust before I return to the pub to pack.

A Conversation around Southern Poetry with Henry Taylor

HENRY TAYLOR: I took a course in Southern literature once, and came out of it mostly with a sense of gratitude that I was writing in the twentieth century. I can't remember a single line by Henry Timrod, and when I think of Sidney Lanier, I usually wonder whether anybody has ever put into a novel a law firm called Habersham and Hall.

Of course the South has been studied at length as a region, maybe more than any other region in the country, and it has been pointed out countless times that it's the only part of the country that was ever defeated in war and occupied by victorious forces. That made a difference between Southerners and other Americans for a long time. It's probably also true that anthologies of Southern poetry are bigger and possibly richer than anthologies of Western poetry or Midwestern poetry; I don't recall seeing an anthology of Northeastern or New England poetry of this century, but it would make an interesting collection, and might be more like a collection of Southern poetry than we might expect.

I guess I'm wondering whether the South's pure size, and the diversity of its cultures, make labels like "Southern poet" almost a matter of geographic origin. There are still Southern poets who use Southern landscapes and speech patterns, but aren't there a great many who don't?

KELLY CHERRY: I suppose that we might approach the Southern poet the same way one approaches God, *via negativa*. In that case, it

seems to me, the Southern poet is, first of all, somebody who is not
a Northern poet. What this means is that the Southern poet is not
unfamiliar with the idea of defeat. The Southern poet is not unfamiliar
with the Bible. The Southern poet is not averse to telling stories, and
may even elect to tell a story rather than expound a point.

I spent part of my childhood in upstate New York, and I remember
being, even then, amazed by the Yankee ability to assume an invul-
nerability, by a Yankee lack of interest in the rhetoric and rhythms
of the King James Bible, and by Yankee reticence. Nobody talked
with anybody! Of course, later on I found out that in New York City
there was quite a lot of talk, but it was nearly all in the form of
argument, not story.

(As for "biblical reference," however, I could not have been happier—though, again, later on—to encounter the splendidly allu-
sive music of such Yankees as Melville, Jonathan Edwards, Robert
Lowell. Even of a Midwesterner like T. S. Eliot. As it happened,
Melville, Edwards, Lowell, and Eliot were not present during my
childhood, in the tenement railway flat we lived in, three flights
above a grocery store.)

These are generalizations and, as such, trivial. Besides, they've
been made before. I've made them before, myself. But what I do
think is peculiar—pretty peculiar—to the Southern poet is the idea of
resurrection. "The idea of resurrection, of the old made new, the last
made first, the dead quickened" underwrites Southern poetry with
a sense of gladness, a sense of irrepressible joy at the possibilities
of reformation, *even* in the face of defeat. *Especially* in the face of
defeat. (The face of defeat could be de sole. I didn't say that.) This
is why, I think, Harold Bloom's theory of misprision—that great
writers must figure out a way to misread their "precursors" in order to
clear imaginative space for themselves—has found so little sympathy
in the South. Southern poets have had no difficulty at all locating
imaginative space for themselves. And how could there ever be any
limit to *imaginative* space?

Consider Fred Chappell. He's taken on Dante, in his long poem,
Midquest. Well, so has James Merrill, but Merrill makes a series

of points, or rather, makes a series of refusals to make a point, while Chappell goes right ahead and tells a bunch of stories. With characters who have names like *Virgil!*

"The Southern poet," I wrote, "who grows up even latterly with the Good News as part of his daily bread, and who is maybe more than some guiltily aware of the need for it, is likely, looking at *the merits of his poetic fathers*, to feel not that anxiety which has been wished on him but an expansive exhilaration."

I wrote that, by the way, back in the days when I was tenaciously clinging to the representative masculine pronoun. I didn't want to sacrifice the power of the singular for the political inclusiveness of a slash mark. If you want to talk about the imaginative space available to women poets, I'll become positively rapturous.

So what I would say is this: there is something beyond geography that defines a Southern poet. Not that you can't be from Japan and know what it is to have lost a war, or from Israel and know the Bible, or from California and have stories to tell, but that these things taken together promote an assertive belief in the possibility of, and need for, self-re-creation.

TAYLOR: I think you're right about the Bible. I was just paging through an anthology of recent Southern poetry, and was surprised at the number of poems that get right to it, very often by way of a story, a recollection, say, of a funeral; the past has an immediacy for many of us. There, now, I've said *us* without thinking, so I have to admit that I can see Southern poets as a group, scattered as we are. I've never even met James Applewhite or Robert Morgan, much as I suspect I would enjoy them if I did. Morgan lives in Ithaca, I think, and that reminds me that a bunch of Southern poets don't live in the South now. We're hardly a Mafia.

CHERRY: But don't you feel that we are at least some sort of extended family? I've never met Robert Morgan, either, and Applewhite only once, but I think of them as literary cousins of a sort. And why? Because they come out of a cultural idiom that parented me, too.

TAYLOR: Do you mean Moon Pies and 7-Elevens? Faulkner and O'Connor? Blues and bluegrass?

CHERRY: Those things are *there*, though for me they are there on the periphery, not at the center, simply because they were not direct influences on my childhood. But no, I mean the larger themes we were talking about.

TAYLOR: Surely, though, Southerners aren't sitting around in a daze of nostalgia, as Northerners seem to think. Not these days.

CHERRY: Hanging out on the metaphorical back porch of a summer evening, memorializing an Arcadian past . . . It's true. I don't know anybody who's doing that. Did Southern writers ever do that?

TAYLOR: I think they did, in the late nineteenth and early twentieth centuries. That may make for some misunderstanding, some misreading. I'm thinking of Andrew Hudgins's *After the Lost War*, which came out a couple of years ago. It's a book-length poem, mostly spoken by Sidney Lanier, but the voice is invented, not based on Lanier's poetry. It's a wonderful book, anything but an exercise in nostalgia.

Progress and nostalgia, Old South and New South; there are tensions there still. Take the question of race. Certainly, in the last thirty or forty years, it has become clear that this is not purely a Southern problem.

CHERRY: That's true. But I, for one Southern writer, do find myself concerned with it in my work, though rather more in my fiction than in my poetry. It's a concern of the novel I have in progress at this moment. But, you know, I'm not sure it's a *Southern* concern. I live now in Madison, Wisconsin, and the race question currently has priority here. Naturally, this finds some expression in my work. Do you feel it's a concern in contemporary poetry by Southerners?

TAYLOR: Yes, but I'm not at all sure that Southern poets deal with it more often than non-Southern poets. The African American poets who are also Southerners have had widely various ways of handling it, or of writing poems in which it is not the subject. I think it's a national question; as such it concerns Southern writers as much as it does anybody else.

But listen: I know you're a Southerner by birth, and largely by upbringing, but I wonder what's Southern about your work. How do you feel about being called a Southern writer?

CHERRY: Much the way I feel about being called a woman writer. That's to say, I don't like any label when it is applied reductively, but there are plenty of things in this world I worry about more. I'm a writer, and I happen to have been born in the South as a woman. I have this weird sense, contrary to all theories of biological or environmental influence, that I could just as well have wound up in a different body in a different place in a different time, but that no matter where I was, I'd still be myself. I don't think there's anything, what, *mystical* about this. I think I just have a very strong sense of myself as, paradoxically, someone able to *lose* herself in other characters. I could almost define myself as someone who can be un-Southern, un-female. Or maybe I mean someone able to *find* herself in other characters. . . . At the same time, I'm well aware of being in this womanly body and living in this time and this place. And you? Do you think of yourself as a Southern man writer?

TAYLOR: Not often. An effect of growing up in a white male society as a white male is that it often takes self-conscious effort to think, "I'm a white male." A complication in my case is that I grew up in rural Virginia, as a Quaker in a Quaker community, and have realized since I was very young that there are contradictions and tensions between those two cultural inheritances. I think those tensions have been more useful to me as a writer than either background alone would have been.

CHERRY: Yes, that's a wonderful thing about the South, wonderful for the Southern writer, at any rate, and not only for the Southern poet. The South is a great place for writers because it is so endlessly rich in contradictions. I've often remarked that I think it is very hard to grow up in the South and *not* become a writer. Those contradictions are so funny, and so tragic, and everywhere. I just published the first book of fiction I've set in the Midwest, and I've been in Wisconsin for going on fourteen years now and had previously spent a couple of winters in southwest Minnesota. I think I had to learn how to see the contradictions in the Midwest before I could write about the Midwest. They are here, of course, but they are subtler. You have to accustom your eye to them. In the American South, contradictions spring up in front of you wherever you go. What Southern writer doesn't find himself, or herself, practically dancing, doing a dance of pure delighted amazement, on every stroll down the street?

TAYLOR: I know what you mean, even though I live where there are roads instead of streets. You remind me, though, that the time I spent living in Salt Lake City, in the late sixties, gave me a place to look back from. I wrote most of the more "Southern" poems in my second book while I was out there. Partly, it was a way of simultaneously combating, and giving in to, the stereotyped assumptions some of my colleagues there made about me. Often, out there, I thought of the trap Jarrell describes in one of his essays; a young Southern woman moves to New York, and people keep saying to her, "Whatever you do, don't lose that precious accent!" and she winds up sounding like Amos 'n' Andy. But probably that's an avoidable pitfall. How does the South look to you from Madison?

CHERRY: Henry, even as we speak I'm looking out at a sidewalk that's got over seventeen inches of snow on it. And you want to know how the South looks to me from here? I'll tell you: From here, the South looks like literature. From here, the South looks like poetry.

On Wisconsin!

I. THE WORLD CREATING ITSELF

It is winter here in Wisconsin, and I am back in my own house. The screens are out and the storm windows in; the cracks have been sealed with rope caulk. Now if I could just get the basement windows boarded up. This is the problem with the basement windows: I slapped insulation in the frames, where there wasn't even glass, but the rain and snow—snow! so soon!—weight this insulation down till it falls inside, lands on the log pile, and I have to start the process all over again. Knowing I'll never learn how to board up the windows myself, I joke that I have three options in this situation: find a husband, win a raise to pay for a handyman, or move south. I think I'm moving south.

Meanwhile, my dog, Duncan, loves the nip in the air. He wags his tail; he tugs impatiently at his leash.

In this weather, Duncan likes to wear a tee-shirt. He has, I shamefacedly admit, a wardrobe of tee-shirts. They're all emblazoned with slogans, of course. (This is a sure indication, I know, that it's too late for me to find a husband.)

One says MALE CHAUVINIST PUPPY.

Another says VERY IMPORTANT POOCH.

A third says SUPERDOG.

His favorite is FIRE HYDRANT INSPECTOR.

I pull the hood of my parka over my head, jangle the keys and rape whistle in my pocket, and off we go, inspecting every fire hydrant in sight. And the fire hydrants are red; the sky is blue; my parka and jeans are blue; my hair is brand-new blonde (for the nonce); and the leaves that Duncan scatters in his wake fly up like butterflies and slowly land, as if making a short migration.

Only to be raked, because a leaf is not a butterfly, and that it is not is what I am thinking about, idly or not so idly, as I hang onto the leash and let Duncan walk me.

The relationship between a leaf and a butterfly, I am thinking to myself, is a metaphorical one, and metaphors, as everyone knows, are the writer's biggest asset. They're her capital, her cash-in-hand, her charge cards; they're what she does business with. And they are made up of words. (We may speak of musical metaphors or visual metaphors, but when we do, we are already, in speaking of them, making an underlying metaphor between music or art and language. A metaphor is a relationship between words.)

But now I see that I began a paragraph by talking about a leaf and a butterfly, and ended it by talking about the words *leaf* and *butterfly*. A leaf became a word.—Or did a word become a leaf?— And a butterfly spelled itself.—Or did a word fly off the blackboard and out an open window?

I think again of the theory according to which writers, overwhelmed by their immediate literary precursors, suffer from "the anxiety of influence." Well, writers *do* suffer from anxiety, from an unsettling and almost—ironically, and by its intrinsic nature—unspeakable anxiety: we cannot trust the very words we possess.

There is—naturally, there would have to be—a fine word for this distrust of language: *misology*. It can be extended to cover a suspicion or downright dislike of argument or any kind of sequential reasoning. But the bottom line is a deeply skeptical attitude toward the word.

It's funny, in a way. The theory of poetic misprision, in reducing the meaning of a poem to the precursor-poem of which it is a necessary misreading, eliminates, when you think about it, the real risks writers run. For this is a theory that eradicates the element of chance from the universe. Its universe of discourse is essentially a Euclidean universe, unaware of the high danger each succeeding writer encounters as she becomes, with maturity, increasingly sensitive to the increasing possibilities for newness, her sheer freedom. Using too glibly Nietzsche's terms "strong" and "weak," the theorist of critical misprision has gotten them confused; he has not yet puzzled out what makes a strong poet strong.

But granting the fact that critics are chronically mislocating meaning, getting it wrong or in the wrong *place*, why would a *writer* distrust the coin in her wallet? A nickel may be less than it was; a word's still a word.

The best way to explain this is to get down to basics. Therefore, while Duncan is decorating the latest fire hydrant, let's imagine we're not outdoors at all: we are indoors, at the table in our study, writing a sentence. *It was a dark and stormy night*, we write, plagiarizing Snoopy (and Bulwer-Lytton). And then what? *And then the doorknob began to turn, ominously.* And then what? *A gloved hand reached in, unfastened the chain lock.* And then? And then?

You could have your protagonist blow her rape whistle.

You could have her husband—in a story, she can have a husband—complainingly ask her why she didn't get up to unlock the door for him.

Her husband could be named Harold Bloom.

(It's a good thing this is fiction we're writing.)

Words will take you anywhere. You can find yourself married, your husband cold, wet, and angry. You can find yourself pleading for a divorce—for your freedom!—or just for a different opening sentence. For someone, including yourself, might give you an opening sentence, and you could write an uncountable number of stories starting just there. Any writer can. That's the exhilaration of it—all those stories and poems out there, just waiting to be discovered. They reveal themselves line by line, paragraph by paragraph, until at last their shape shines as brightly as Madison's Lake Mendota on a sunny day in early winter.

This is no theory of artistic inspiration. The words don't find you; you have to go looking for them. But one leads to another, and that to another, and the next thing you know, you have run out of bread crumbs, and the birds have eaten the ones you already dropped, and you are somewhere you never expected to be: on page 5, or 15, or 500.

It's exhilarating, but it's also lonesome and frightening out here in the woods. And how did we get here? We were in my basement; we went for a walk; we were writing in my study; and now we're in the forest that has tempted us, taunted us, held us since childhood, the forest where the butterflies are falling from trees, and leaves are rising from the ground and flying southward in flocks.

Did you know that some butterflies return every year to precisely the same branch on the same tree in, of all places, Bolivia? They fold up their wings for the night, the way we put on our pajamas. Dreaming on their branch, they're called Sleeping Assemblies.

Of course writers distrust words. They call to us; we follow them. We learn to listen to them, to hear what our own written words tell us, and they tell us when we have strayed, when we are on target, when we are getting there. But you have to be wary of anything with that much power over you. In fact, the more self-conscious the writer becomes, and perhaps, at the same time, the more self-mocking or pugilistic in relation to language (for this is the recent history of much fiction and poetry), the harder the writer works to establish control, not only over the language but over herself as well. You work and work to redress the balance; you master your craft, you learn technique, you learn courage. The word can still lord it over you, anytime it wants.

Are these words there in that forest from all time, then, awaiting discovery? Are they eternal, and do they live in some Platonic realm awaiting the writer's discovery? Was there a Big Bang, and the Logos shattered into a lot of little *logoi*, and did all the words that exist pool together and freeze over in that realm of the Perfect, like Lake Mendota, and are we writers skating figure eights forever around the same limited dictionary?

No. Words beget words, and language is as organic as life. Malthus has nothing on Webster. Why should any writer be anxious about running out of words? We have the ones that have been given to us; and we have the new ones we are making today; and our successors will have yet another world with yet more words in it with which to write.

Words are not fixed or frozen; neither are they in flight. They are the known leading to the unknown, and they are the unknown making themselves known. Words are the *world's* mind thinking itself into being.

And so, I don't *need* insulation, I think, calling Duncan to heel and heading home. I don't need a husband. I almost don't even need a raise. My very next sentence may take me south—or to Germany, Bolivia, Timbuktu.

II. FAITH AND SIGNIFICATION

And so, I went to Cleveland. There I had the pleasure of serving as writer-in-residence at Cleveland State University; it *was* a pleasure, because the students cared about writing. These students asked firmly worded questions, they listened attentively, and they had the highest sophistication there is, the sophistication of being unafraid of their own enthusiasm. They had advanced far beyond wanting to be writers and wanted only to write, and they brought what they had written to me for my response.

But on the plane back to Madison, here where I live and work between such trips, I wondered what these students would take away from my visit. I was taking myself away; what were they taking away? No doubt being airborne heightens anyone's desire for panoramic answers.

I went to my office. It was a Saturday morning; it was eight o'clock. There was no one in the halls. Later on, an occasional graduate student would surface, to grade term papers for Survey of Lit 208, or to work on a dissertation. I set my coffee and doughnuts down on the slide-out tray of my desk and began to go through the week's accumulation of mail. As I read it, my thoughts veered again to the students in Cleveland, whom I had so recently spoken to and with. What had I done to them, suggesting that a life of writing could ever bring them joy, or contentment, or fulfillment, or even free weekends?

Therefore, if I did not say it then, let me say it now: A life of writing will bring you none of these things. It will bring you grief; it will annoy your friends; it will drive spouses away, or batty; it will turn the calendar pages more relentlessly than you ever dreamt. Writing is hazardous to your health. Sylvia Plath wanted too much to be a writer.

Let me now say this to those wonderful students I met at Cleveland: You must advance even further than beyond the stage of wanting to be a writer. You must, though no one may yet have told you this, actually throw away the time-honored distinction between wanting to write and wanting to be a writer; you must throw away the *wanting*. Remember that every time you write anything at all, even if it goes unread forever, or even if, as is sometimes worse, it is read but not responded to as you had hoped—remember that, as words are signs, *the act of writing is a sign*. It points to something beyond itself.

What does the act of writing signify? That you, the writer, have an inner life, that you are more than what you appear to be, regardless of what that may be, that you possess spirit, imagination, thought, that the world of the immaterial is housed in you. And that you believe others—others who might, in an ideal world, be readers—possess these attributes as well. The act of writing is an act of faith.

You must believe in the possibility of the imagination to transform what is dispiritingly bland to beauty, chaos to order, senselessness to sense, what sickens and appalls to energy and hope, and in short, the unbearable to the, believe it or not, bearable. Our manuscripts, published or not, are the signs of our faith; they witness to it, and they are therefore essential to it. It may be that the world can do without our manuscripts; faith cannot.

Faith depends for its very existence on our writing.

Is this not amazing? I mean, is this not *amazing?*

Note that it is not true that writing *depends* on faith (work has been written from despair); it is *faith* that depends on, that lives on, that feeds on writing. (But, as has been said before about faith, without it, the work is nothing; with it, the work is everything.)

This is what I meant to say to the students in Cleveland; this is what I hope they took away from my visit. To write is to witness to our humanity. A reviewer, a publisher can evaluate the written word; no reviewer, no publisher, not even any writer-in-a-one-week-residence can evaluate the act of writing, for the act of writing, as an act of faith, is purely beyond evaluation: it is invaluable.

Believe it.

III. WHERE *IS* THE WORLD?

As I was saying, words can take us anyplace, even Cleveland. Words can convey us coast to coast in the time it takes to write a subordinate clause—and without losing our luggage. Language is cheaper than airfare.

Many years ago I read an interview with a writer who was making this same point. "Why go to Brazil to rob a bank," the writer asked, although probably not in exactly those words, "when I can stay here and rob the bank in my novel?" For that writer, "here" was France. It is less trouble to stay at home, even in France, than it is to go to Brazil. The writer who robs a bank in a novel is less likely to get caught than anyone who robs a bank in Brazil.

Recently, I myself have robbed a real estate firm in Bolivia; I have dug for fossils in the Red Beds outside Bloemfontein in South Africa; I have survived—and I was the only member of the team who did—a scientific expedition in Siberia in 1913.

What plane flies to 1913?

There is the question of research. Why should anyone believe what I say about Bolivia, the Red Beds, or a scientific expedition in Siberia in 1913? Our English teachers in high school cautioned us, did they not, "to write about what we know." But for one thing, I wanted to write *what* I knew, not *about* what I knew, and for another, I was, I further admit, drawn to write not only what I knew but what I did *not* know. Pen and paper, the typewriter, the word processor are not mere recording devices; they are the writer's vehicles for exploration; they are airplanes and automobiles, the Queen Elizabeth II, a dogsled. They are magic carpets. The writer enters her study the way an astronaut climbs into her spaceship, with a sense of rising excitement, with pleasure in her own mastery of the control panel, with a finger itching to launch into hyperdrive. I have been to the moon; time warps are nothing.

Another interview, another writer: Saul Bellow was asked, "Then you aren't especially disturbed by readers of *Henderson [the Rain King]*, for example, who say that Africa really isn't like that?"

"Years ago," Bellow answered, "I studied African ethnography with the late Professor Herskovits. Later he scolded me for writing a book like *Henderson*. He said the subject was much too serious for such fooling. I felt that my fooling was fairly serious."

My fooling is fairly serious.

I look up facts. I read Bolivian history and botany and biology. I read about African geography and politics to locate elements transportable to South America, to the entirely special situation I am establishing in South America. I develop a card file on NASA. Weirdly, perhaps, I know all about glyptodonts, green mambas, mammoths, and the way the planet Earth looks from various points of distance and angle. I study what I don't know until it becomes what I know. At that precise instant, I am ready to take off.

Where? Into *the unknowable*. For—and this is important—it is not the unknown that beckons; it is *the unknowable*, the landscape that exists only in the imagination, that cannot be discovered until it is created, that writes its singular history in the process of pushing itself into being, paragraph by paragraph, sentence by sentence, word by word.

Say I send a couple of basically sweet-tempered revolutionaries named Miguel and Ramón into Santa Cruz to hold up the Euro-Bolivian Real Estate and Livestock Co., and they pull off a coup that gathers speed for three hundred double-spaced manuscript pages and crosses oceans and continents. I tag along; I'm in Bolivia, New York, Oklahoma, London, the Vatican. The Vatican? For writers, the shortest distance between any two points is a verb.

But there is a risk in all this, even for the writer. If they get caught, Miguel and Ramón have to take the heat for the robbery. (Read the book to find out if they do.) The writer runs another risk.

The writer runs the risk of losing the world he lives in. Indeed, if he writes long enough, hard enough, and well enough, he runs the risk of forgetting what world he does live in.

I tried to explain this, once upon a time, to some colleagues in the psychology department. "I live in imaginary worlds," I said to them; "I make up worlds and move right in." I do believe they thought this was crazy, but any writer knows very well that I was only describing the writer's trade. What would be crazy would be to try to make up a world *without* moving in, because it is the moving in that creates that world. You have to visit a place in order to put it on the map. The late Professor Herskovits was not wrong; he merely failed to understand the sense in which he was right.

Imagine—if I may put it that way—forgetting where you live. Imagine concentrating so intensely that you call a new world into existence—and misplace your own. You could live out your life as an alien, a monster on a foreign and inhospitable shore, lonely and unloved. The characters you have created will come to distrust you: they have no more need of you. You are a misfit, a stranger in a world you made, and the better you have made it, the less room there is in it for you. You take to living behind rocks, venturing forth only at night; you live on the scraps of food your characters throw out after supper—you raid your own characters' garbage pails. Imagine running this risk every day.

Every day, you go into *the unknowable*. It is not getting there that's difficult; it is coming home. "Write about what you know," the English teacher always says, adding that we always know "about" our backyard. Let me ask you something: what do you know, truly know, about your backyard?

No, the way home is not easy. It requires yet another act of the imagination; you have to reinvent your backyard.

I quit my desk; I go downstairs; I am in search of facts about my backyard. I keep notes in a file folder labeled "Reality."

I discover that "here" is not France.

Peering out the window of the back door, I see that Duncan has his nose shoved through the wire-mesh dog pen. Mr. Mani from across the way is leaning over the fence, scratching Duncan behind the ears. I know that no matter what the dog-psychologists would say, Duncan only appears to be in his dog pen; really, he is in heaven. And he's not even a writer.

Duncan and I are pack animals; we hang out together.

I call him in. I slip his leash over his head, which he bows patiently. The only time he ever bows his head patiently, of course, is when I am slipping his leash over it.

I'm glad that Duncan is not imaginary.

We go out the front way. I open the door and bam! light slams into my eyes. The high hedge is greening; the tulips blaze against my brick house; hyacinths glow.

Duncan pulls at his leash and calls me to heel. We race down the steps to the sidewalk. All along Highland, the telephone wires whistle good news: the world is where you find it.

A House in the Desert

RECENTLY I WENT TRAIL-RIDING in the foothills of the Tucson mountains.
I was riding Butch, a chestnut of narrow girth. He was quick and
light, and riding him, I felt close to the ground.

The wrangler had said she would take me to a place I had not
been before. We rode through the dry wash. Saguaro skeletons rotted
on the desert floor. A thin wipe of cloud spilled across the blue sky.
There were roadrunners and jackrabbits. Inca doves cooed. Barrel
cactus, hedgehog cactus, teddy bear cactus, pincushion cactus, and
creosote bushes, which emit a sweet but pungent odor when wet, live
in the desert. The wrangler said that she feels the cacti are friends,
each as individual as any person. She has named many of them.
"Fred," she will say, as we climb past a young saguaro, one as yet
unarmed. "This is Fred." Saguaros grow to be very old; they may be
fifty before they develop a single arm.

The sun fell on my arms. I was warm, and pushed up my sleeves.
Butch blew through his nostrils.

After a while, picking our way over loose rock and bleached twigs,
we entered a place I had never been. "There was a house here," the
wrangler said.

I didn't understand what she meant. After all, I was a tenderfoot. I
looked around, and seeing the outlines of a house laid on the ground,
I thought I was looking at the foundation of a house. I thought perhaps
someone had started to build a house here and had abandoned it.

Something I said revealed my confusion. "It's an imaginary house,"
the wrangler explained. She had come down from Canada, and her

voice had a quiet, clipped quality, as if it were somehow angular. But she was round, red-haired, and freckled.

She continued: "It happened while I was away. I had gone back to Canada, and my visit stretched into months. They hired a girl here, a retarded girl, to help with the housework. Her name was Laurie."

I asked if Laurie had really been retarded, or was it rather that she had some psychological difficulty. I was always retarded when it came to applying the appellation "retarded." I felt *slow* did not mean *stupid* and in fact sometimes meant *smart*.

"I guess I don't really know," the wrangler said. "But they called her Crazy Laurie. She used to write mash notes to Josephine and leave them on her desk." Josephine worked in the ranch's main office, and she was married to a foreman at the copper mine.

"What did Josephine do?"

"Well, I wasn't here. But I don't think she did anything. What could she have done?" The wrangler pointed at a spot on the ground. "Here is a closet," she said. "And over there—that's a semicircular driveway."

It was as large as a driveway.

"Yes," the wrangler said. "It is a full-sized house. There's the hearth, and there's a garden." She showed me how the plants had been imported, and how the walkways and driveway had been outlined with rocks and picked clean of rocks. Desert air doesn't corrode, or does so only so slowly that time seems motionless. A car swept down the wash in a flood will stay unrusted, chrome bright and shiny, for years afterward. Nothing had disturbed this house's careful outlines.

"I've told them, back at the ranch," the wrangler said, "about this house. They say that Laurie used to talk about her house in the desert. Everyone thought she was just making it up. But here it is. It is a *real* imaginary house. She used to make furniture, too, the kind of furniture you can make from cacti."

"Maybe she planned to furnish her house," I said.

"Maybe. Look, I mean, just *look* at all that—" The wrangler waved a hand. She wore a red cardigan. "Do you remember when you were a child, and you used to make houses out of anything?"

I remembered that my sister and I used to turn chairs on their sides and throw blankets over them, creating rooms. Sometimes we built whole cities. We liked to pretend we lived in Baghdad or Singapore.

"Laurie must have done that. She must have come up here at night—because no one ever saw her, and we aren't far from the bunkhouse—and worked on her house, and sat in it and dreamed of walls and windows. What could she have been thinking of?"

As we rode back to the ranch, the sun slid down the sky, like a child on a playground slide. The lights of Tucson were white in the still-light sky. There was snow on Mt. Lemmon.

Butch shied, coming downhill, then settled into an easy walk through the wash. I held the reins in my right hand. The wrangler was in front.

The wrangler was riding a palomino. The air was so pure it seemed like a mirror in which the palomino was reflected like a flash of golden sun.

I thought about Laurie and her house in the desert. One day, near the close of the season, she had asked the chef to take her north with him. He had a cabin in Minnesota.

He said no, and the next day, she was gone. She must have hitched a ride with someone. I thought she might have been frantic to escape from a hopeless love—hasn't everyone, at some time, felt that crushing panic? In any case, no one heard from her. She sent no more love letters to Josephine. No one had known where she came from, and now no one knew where she had gone. No wonder she had wanted so desperately to lay a foundation, defining herself in space and time.

Laurie had sited her house with great shrewdness. From its front room, the view was panoramic; from the ranch, its location was invisible.

What had she thought of, those long, solitary evenings in the desert? What sequence of ideas had tracked its way through that slow, shrewd brain? What does it mean to be retarded or crazy?

I could not imagine then. I can't now. What can we say of the intelligence, or imagination, when we do not even know what someone, anyone, thinks?

Writing about Running

A FORMER STUDENT OF MINE, A PHYSICIST who worked in Malaysia during the early days of his retirement and now, in these latter days, spends his time viewing films about birth in order to learn about death, attending poetry readings, and writing splendid letters, wrote to me.

"Did you know," my student wrote, "that Teller lost a foot while running to catch the bus?"

My student had been at the University of Chicago when Edward Teller was Professor of Physics there. Teller was "the father of the hydrogen bomb."

I once studied some physics myself, although I studied more mathematics. But I had never known that Teller lost a foot while running to catch the bus.

Where was he going?

Why was he in such a hurry? Couldn't he have waited for the next bus? Was he headed for work, for home? Was there a family crisis? Had he gotten *off* the bus and then remembered that he'd left his notes *on* it?

These questions intrigue me, and I am pleased to think about them because I feel no need whatever to go look up the right answers. I am sorry that Teller lost his foot, but I am glad that I don't need to worry about why he lost it. In this instance, knowing how is sufficient.

Knowing how, I can imagine all kinds of answers. Any one of them will do. All of them will do, if I like, since I can arrive at a different conclusion every day of the week, and not one of those conclusions need be tested against reality. I do not need to look up the facts behind Teller's loss of his foot. I do not even need to know whether it was his right foot or his left.

I do not even need to know whether my student has remembered the incident accurately. It does not matter if it was in fact Fermi who lost his foot, or Rabi, or Bethe. Or if it happened not in Chicago but in Los Alamos, or Berkeley, or Oak Ridge. Or if it wasn't a bus but a cab. Or if what he was really running after was a girl.

(It might matter if it was a girl. That might change the story significantly.)

Still, the point is that ever since my student wrote me about Teller's losing a foot while running to catch the bus, I have had great pleasure (at the expense of someone else's pain, unfortunately) thinking about the different circumstances that might have led to this event.

I have often wondered just how fast the bus was going, and how fast, or how slowly, Teller was running.

We have here, perhaps, a whole new approach to the theory of relativity. Was Teller too slow to catch the bus? Had he gotten paunchy, a bit thick around the waist? Was his cholesterol too high? Or was the bus going too fast? Or were they both traveling at a rate projected to provide collision without trauma, even allowing a margin for error, when the bus, introducing the unfigurable factor of chance, took a corner too sharply? Who is to say? A judge, the insurance agent, the driver, Teller. Any point of view is possible. It is possible to have a point of view without even being a witness to the event. I have my own point of view—any one I choose to have—and I was nowhere near the accident.

That is one of the reasons for being a writer. You get to look at the world from any point of view that interests you. You can take a seat on the bus and press your face to the window, hoping the strange, frantic man who was shouting and running just before he stumbled, as it appears he has done, has not been badly hurt. Or you can run alongside him, finally falling behind, giving up and shrugging exaggeratedly so everyone can see you realize how foolish you have looked, and then forgetting yourself as you watch, with horror, while the man ahead of you gets his foot squished under the huge tire.

You can be Teller himself, in shock, wondering what has happened.

Is that your foot in the gutter? Is it wearing the same shoe you put on it that morning before you left for work? Is it really wearing *a red sock?*

Will the world now be forever unbalanced, off center? Has the Earth in its orbit been *hobbled?*

For here are the facts, which I have not been able, in the end, to resist looking up:

- It was not a bus but a streetcar.
- It was not Chicago but Munich.
- Teller was still a student, in his twenties.
- The world *had* gone permanently aslant, and all of Europe was sliding under an onrushing streetcar.

I remember running once. I was working at the Virginia Center for the Creative Arts. The Center is a place where writers, musicians, and artists can live for a time free from distraction; I was happy to be there, but I worked so much, seated at a typewriter, that I had to take short breaks—five or ten minutes at a time—to lie on the floor to realign my back. Two women writers, friends I'd made at the Center, suggested I join them on their morning runs; they said running would help my back.

The next morning I rose while the dew was still on the grass. The air was fragrant with magnolia and clover and with the world's best smell, box elder. Mist hung over the cow pasture. Honeysuckle wound its way over the fence. Rhododendron lined the road.

We ran along a dirt road from the house past the studios; then the road became a paved road; then we ran across a meadow padded with daisies and dandelions.

But my feet hurt. My face was sweating. My tee-shirt was plastered to my back, and my back was sorer than ever. Martha and Myra had pulled out in front and were racing away from me, and whenever I looked after them, the sun, jogging over the hills, felt like something thrown or blasted into my eyes, felt like acid or buckshot. Too, the salt in my own sweat stung my eyes. The road—by turns paved and unpaved, asphalt, dirt, gravel, or grass—slammed against my feet as if someone were whacking my soles with a cane. I veered off, ran up the steps to the house, ran through the front room, ran through the hallway, ran into the kitchen, and collapsed.

I could hardly breathe. I clung to the sink, drinking great gulps of air. After a while, I was able to drink some water. I ran the water until it was as cold as it could get, and drank some more of it, and thought, *This is the world's best water.*

I was still dizzy. I found my way out to the dining room, sat down, and my blurred vision began to clear. The room came into focus. I looked at my feet. I was wearing blue sneakers. Dimestore sneakers. I still had both feet.

I went upstairs to my room, rested for a while—lying on the floor to realign my back—and then put on a clean pair of socks and some sandals. Then I walked to my studio. I walked slowly. It was full morning now. There were gnats and mosquitoes. I didn't run from them; I walked at my own pace.

In my studio, I sat down at my typewriter. There I was, sedentary again. Suddenly I felt wonderful. This, I thought, was the proper position for a writer. Writers should not run. They should sit at their desks and write.

Sitting at a desk, writing, may not be a wise way to live one's life. I happen to think it may be wise, but I am not, here, arguing that it is. But is running after a bus a wise way to live one's life?

Wisely or not, I gave up running that day. My two friends covered miles. I regretted not being able to keep up with them, but no one can do everything. Teller couldn't even catch the damn bus.

Well, streetcar.

The world limps under the weight of its own history, and imagination is a prosthetic device.

Prosthesis: the addition of a sound or syllable to a word.

Or say that the world is a text that needs, always and again, careful footnoting if it is not to stumble into hopeless nonsense, amputated forever from the given of the past, the promise of the future. I think I'm holding my own, sitting here, not going anywhere, writing in place.

The Two Cultures at the End
of the Twentieth Century

AN ESSAY ON POETRY AND SCIENCE

IN HIS ESSAY "THE TWO CULTURES," first published in the *New Statesman* in 1956 and later included in a series of lectures delivered at Cambridge University, C. P. Snow said of himself, "By training I was a scientist: by vocation I was a writer. . . . It was a piece of luck, if you like, that arose through coming from a poor home." I, too, came from a poor home, though it was an educated home, and my parents, who were string quartet violinists, thought that economic salvation would lie in having one of their children turn out to be a scientist. I never got further than a hodgepodge of introductory science courses and rather more math, but even that superficial acquaintance with science has proved to be "a piece of luck." I have taken seriously what C. P. Snow called the problem of "the two cultures"—that "the intellectual life of the whole of western society is increasingly being split into two polar groups"—and tried to find ways in my writing to reunite what had been separated, to bring together what had been estranged, to fuse, as it were, what had been fissioned. If the results are essentially private, well, that is because those scientists and scholars over there on the other side of the chasm need to get busy and do *their* part, by, of course, reading some contemporary poetry.

C. P. Snow may seem an unfashionable figure by now; he's probably unknown to most younger people. Despite his many novels, none of my writing students has ever heard of him. But there was a time when, in the heat of the Cold War, in the Race to Space, his essay came as a call to arms. In October, 1957, Sputnik went up—and C. P. Snow's analysis of "the two cultures" was thought to have been prophetic. Thus it was that some time later, at the age of seventeen, I found myself a sophomore at the New Mexico Institute of Mining and Technology. My being a student at a mining school, precisely because it *was* such a ridiculous thing for me to be, is a good indication of the values the country held at that time. I recall sitting in a classroom with mining students and young engineers, budding atmospheric physicists and possibly a future oil magnate or two, taking an I.Q. test for spatial perspective. Thousands of miles from my home in Virginia, wearing East Coast hemlines that were shockingly short in the fifties Southwest, I chewed on my pencil and tried to figure out how many hidden sides a two-dimensional object might possess. I believe I had the lowest I.Q. ever recorded at New Mexico Tech.

All the same, like loving a man the world has said you may not marry, I lived in a kind of constant scientific swoon, ravished by the beauty of mathematics, the complicated narrative of paleontology, the diagrams of vectors in our physics notebooks, Mondrian in their clarity.

If spatial configurations were not my forte, temporal ones may have been. Even before I read C. P. Snow, I liked almost nothing better, during high school, than to listen to the Beethoven quartets, which are the most beautiful explorations of time ever conducted in music, late at night while drawing up charts of geologic eras and periods at my desk. I had an attic room, with dormer windows. You could listen to music there without disturbing the rest of the house. And so, late at night, the whole house was sound asleep—sleeping sound; sound, sleeping—except for my room, which was wakeful with sublime music and the meditation of time, that long line next to which my own life, at fourteen, was not so much as a visible dot.

Some of the images of those nights that I spent lost in time returned to me as I was working on my book of poetry *Natural Theology.* I chose to open this book with a poem titled "Phylogenesis," and

perhaps, as I wrote it, I was remembering the vivid intellectual
fantasies of my youth:

> She cracks her skin
> like a shell, and goes in
>
> She camps in her womb
> She sucks the marrow from her bones
>
> and sips bison's blood
> in the afternoon; for years,
>
> snow piles outside the cave she burrows in
> She wakes to warm weather,
>
> fur on her four feet, grass
> rising and falling in waves like water
>
> She feeds on flowering plants,
> enjoys a cud of orchid and carrot
>
> In the Middle Permian, scales slippery as shale appear
> on her back; her spine unfurls a sail broadside
>
> to the sun, filling with a light like wind, while *Sphenodon*
> turns its third eye on the sky, sensing
>
> rain, and rock salt washes into the ocean
> Silent as mist, she slides down a mud bank on her underbelly
>
> Lobe-finned and fleshy,
> she pumps air through her gills
>
> She's soft as jelly
> Her skull is limestone
>
> She drifts, like a continent
> or a protozoan, on the planet's surface,
>
> and sinks into the past
> like a pebble into a brackish pool

The seas catch fire
The earth splits and gapes

The earth cracks open like an egg
and she goes in

We begin

Whatever else may be said about that poem, I am pretty sure that it is the only poem ever to get into it a reference to *Sphenodon*, a predecessor of the modern lizard. I hope that this is a scientific enough reference to appease the spirit of C. P. Snow. After complaining that "[i]t is bizarre how very little of twentieth-century science has been assimilated into twentieth-century art," he admitted wryly that, at least, "[n]ow and then one used to find poets conscientiously using scientific expressions, and getting them wrong—there was a time when 'refraction' kept cropping up in verse in a mystifying fashion, and when 'polarised light' was used as though writers were under the illusion that it was a specially admirable kind of light." And I know that when black holes began to be talked about in *Time* and *Newsweek*, they were suddenly cropping up in poems everywhere (mine too), as if the mere importation of a scientific term into a poem were enough to freight the poem with new meaning. It isn't, of course.

No, the challenge of using science in poetry lies in using it in a way that results in stronger poetry, a poetry that incorporates as much as possible of the real world. One contemporary poet who has been much drawn to the bleak romance of astronomy as a way of training a telescope on the real world we live in is Robert Watson. In certain of his poems we come to know an astronomer's stubborn love for space itself, as if the distance between two objects were more seductive than any mere object itself could be. "This is a universe of luck and chance," Watson writes in "The Radio Astronomer," and continues, "Galaxies / Spin in flight like snow, rattle in space, are gone."

In another poem, "Riding in Space I Kiss My Wife," he allows us to view a more mundane romance through the lens of the speaker's romance with the "universe of luck and chance," so that we see our messy, mortal world as if from very far away, from as far away as cosmic unconcern:

> Over us in bed together kissing,
> The night rides,
> Dumps a splintered ice-boat, its shrouds,
> The universe in our bed, our children's beds.
> The arteries of heaven run bursting with cars.
> "There are billions of galaxies," I read,
> "And a galaxy contains countless billions of stars."

Watson's use of astronomical imagery heightens, brilliantly, the sense of despair in his poems; it extends despair, the sense of overwhelming distance between actuality and ideal, into a lyricism of the first magnitude.

The poet and fiction writer R. H. W. Dillard, whose vocabularies of reference are astonishingly varied and knowledgeably detailed, encompassing, among others, science, cinema, literature, art, and linguistics, takes as an epigraph the philosopher of process A. N. Whitehead's pronunciamento, "The stable universe is slipping away from under us," to enter a poem, "March Again," about the fixity of love:

> Christ could have swum away
> From the cross on air,
> But he chose to be nailed
> To the ground. You grow dizzy
> And each step is like walking
> On water. . . .

Reading Whitehead, the writer has recognized in an idea about the world something that can be employed not only as hypothesis or conclusion but as a way of thinking, an approach to *another* idea. This, after all, is central to what writers, I believe, want to do. They don't want just to embellish the world with images, decking the world's hall with bough after bough of holly. They want to lead the reader through the hall into all the rooms that lie beyond. A way to get to those rooms is by using an *idea* as an image.

For instance, in the long poem, "A Bird's-Eye View of Einstein," that closes my collection *Relativity: A Point of View*, I turned to the theory of relativity as a way of thinking about the Trinity, three-in-one, and especially about the Trinity as it might manifest itself—or its selves—to a woman's point of view. There is a phrase, "duets with Einstein," that might seem to the uninitiated to be the whole of my use of the theory of relativity in that poem but in fact the whole poem is predicated on the theory, presenting, as it does, a series of parallel triads through which the point of view slides in a very strange way, bending the time of the poem back on itself like reflected—or possibly refracted, and maybe even polarized—light.

Still, what the poet wants to make of science is not more science but more poetry. I have to admit that I am not always bothered by an excessive need to be factual (though I hope, always and forever, to be truthful). In a longish narrative poem I tried to imagine a scientific expedition in Siberia in 1913. I have no idea whether an expedition like the one in the poem ever actually took place, and yet an encounter with a prehistoric creature that has been frozen during an Ice Age to reemerge into life thousands of years later certainly recurs again and again as a kind of unarticulated myth, and so I decided to articulate it. I picked the year 1913 out of the historical air, to increase the tension: World War I is about to begin; the Russian Revolution is waiting in the wings. Readers have asked me about the paleobotanist who appears in the poem and is named Szymanowski. There may well be a paleobotanist named Szymanowski, but I have never read of him. The only Szymanowski I know of was a Polish violinist, and I know of him only because, finding myself in need of a name that would provide a satisfying mouthful of syllables in my poem, I raced downstairs—I was visiting my parents at the time—and asked my father what he could suggest. My father, not having read C. P. Snow, seized upon what he knew best and came up with the name "Szymanowski." I believe that if I had just stayed downstairs he could have found me a violinist's name that would do for every occupation I might ever have literary occasion to refer to. I ran with

"Szymanowski" back to my room and stuck it into my poem. What is important, sometimes, is the scheme of science rather than the science itself, although I suspect the scheme will not likely occur to writers who don't regularly include science as one of the things they think about. For example, in a poem about the rose, which I wanted to convey in all its traditional romantic, theological, and literary dimensions, I took a botanical lecture as my model for the poem's form. Each description that the poem gives of "the rose" is presented as a definition, as if something scientifically taxonomic were going on, which, of course, it is not:

THE ROSE

A botanical lecture

It's the cup of blood,
the dark drink lovers sip,
the secret food

It's the pulse and elation
of girls on their birthdays,
it's good-byes at the railroad station

It's the murmur of rain,
the blink of daylight
in a still garden, the clink
of crystal; later, the train

pulling out, the white cloth,
apples, pears, and champagne—
good-bye! good-bye!
We'll weep petals, and dry
our tears with thorns

A steep country springs up beyond
the window, with a sky like a pond,

a flood. It's a rush
of bright horror, a burning bush,

night's heart,
the living side of the holy rood

It's the whisper of grace in the martyrs' wood

Writing that poem, I felt as though having access to the *idea*, at least, of a botanical lecture gave me a new route into an otherwise familiar place, arguably even an overtrafficked place, in the land of poetic symbolism. It gave me a new take on an old problem. It worries me that so many writing students confine themselves to the study of literature—and literature in English, at that. Obviously, writers need to know their own literatures as well as possible, but that is not all they need to know. I think it is unfortunate for students that so many of them are now able to earn college degrees without taking serious courses in science and math (and let's throw classical literature in there while we are at it). There is a world out there to be written about.

Because, the truth is, I am an empiricist at heart and I do believe that there is a world out there but that it is a world difficult to know. I believe we must bring every instrument at our disposal to bear on the knowing of it. And science is one of those instruments, but so is literature. Literature is not merely an ornament or a therapy; it is a way of knowing the world. This is what *scientists* need to understand about *literature*.

(I will go even further, all the way out on a theoretical limb, and state that different forms of literature are essentially different modes of perception, though each form partakes to some degree of the others: fiction is the way we come to know the world of relation; the personal essay is the way we come to know—more than the subject of its discussion—the mind of the essayist, how thinking occurs; poetry, for all the use it makes of emotion, is the way we come to know the thing itself, the simple undeniable fact of existence, of existence in all its manifold particularity.)

If it is clear that literature (and other art) is a kind of knowledge, it is equally clear that math and science are forms of beauty, to anyone who will recognize them as such. I will never forget that day in a classroom at the University of Virginia when Ian Hacking was attempting to explain to a group of graduate students Gödel's proof of the impossibility of establishing the presence of internal logical consistency in deductive systems. Some of the students were working on their doctorates in mathematics; others of us were philosophy students dazed by the entire mad enterprise of mathematical logic, and for weeks we had been wondering how we were ever going to get out of this class alive. Hacking went to the blackboard and proceeded to work his way around the room until all four walls were white with chalked equations constituting an abbreviated version of the proof. And suddenly, I went from being dazed to being dazzled, as everything revealed itself to me. It was a vision, surely, not unlike the moment of illumination I experienced when, at five, I finally, after great effort, learned how to tie my shoelaces—but that was a triumph too, a door opening onto a universe of pattern and intricacy and scope. It was like reading Shakespeare or listening to Beethoven. It was beauty, pure and simple, or not so simple, and if I no longer remember anything I ever knew of mathematical logic, I have never forgotten the sheer gorgeousness of it. This is what *writers* need to understand about *mathematics and science.*

Two books of poetry published in the seventies spoke directly to the writer's responsibility to understand what he can of mathematics and science. John Bricuth, in *The Heisenberg Variations*, an extremely interesting and often very funny collection, evokes a contemporary sense of uncertainty, our sense that we are probably, right now, the butt of a joke we don't quite get. Here is "Talking Big":

> We are sitting here at dinner talking big.
> I am between the two dullest men in the world
> Across from the fattest woman I ever met.
> We are talking big. Someone has just remarked
> That energy equals the speed of light squared.
> We nod, feeling that that is "pretty nearly correct."
> I remark that the square on the hypotenuse can more
> Than equal the squares on the two sides. The squares

> On the two sides object. The hypotenuse over the way
> Is gobbling the grits. We are talking big. The door
> Opens suddenly revealing a vista that stretches
> To infinity. Parenthetically, someone remarks
> That a body always displaces its own weight.
> I note at the end of the gallery stands a man
> In a bowler and a black coat with an apple where
> His head should be, with his back to me, and it is me.
> I clear my throat and re (parenthetically) mark
> That a body always falls of its own weight.
> "whoosh-WHOOM!" sighs the hypotenuse across,
> And (godknows) she means it with all her heart.

Who are the squares on the two sides, if not ourselves? And we are talking big, but no matter how big, "a body always displaces its own weight." Who is the man in the bowler and black coat? Traditionally Death, he is also, here, the speaker in the poem, who will displace his own weight. Does he also represent the death of the Newtonian universe, those reasonable laws displaced by the apple of relativity? And is the apple also the apple of the knowledge of good and evil? Oh, the poet *meant* it when he said, "We are talking big."

Al Zolynas, in *The New Physics*, takes an opposite tack, turning to the unseen structures of subatomic physics to comment on our daily life in the middle range. His book is divided into three sections, "Color," "Charm," and "Strangeness," as if the most minuscule particles of the world, quarks, were also metaphors for it. In the title poem, a prose poem, he explains his method:

> And so, the closer he looks at things, the farther away they seem. At dinner, after a hard day at the universe, he finds himself slipping through his food. His own hands wave at him from beyond a mountain of peas. Stars and planets dance with molecules on his fingertips. After a hard day with the universe, he tumbles through himself, flies through the dream galaxies of his own heart. In the very presence of his family he feels he is descending through an infinite series of Chinese boxes.
>
> This morning, when he entered the little broom-closet of the electron looking for quarks and neutrinos, it opened into an immense hall, the

hall into a plain—the Steppes of Mother Russia! He could see men hauling barges up the river, chanting faintly for their daily bread.

It's not that he longs for the old Newtonian Days, although something of plain matter and simple gravity might be reassuring, something of the good old equal-but-opposite forces. And it's not that he hasn't learned to balance comfortably on the see-saw of paradox. It's what he sees in the eyes of his children—the infinite black holes, the ransomed light at the center.

What we want to know, what we crave to know, is, of course, the answer to the oldest questions: Why are we—even our children—made to die? Why must the good suffer? Can we be good? Why should we be good? Is there point or purpose to our existence? These are the questions both scientists and poets would like to know the answers to. If none has yet fathomed a single answer, we may acknowledge that the questions themselves compose a kind of Rosetta stone. Asking the same questions in our different languages of science and art, we learn to translate ourselves into one another, we see that we are different words for the same humanity. There is a vision of oneness here, amid the many voices in which the universe speaks its own being. In "The Study of Ecology," Dillard says that Thoreau, examining the veins of leaves against sunlight,

> Also looked at his hand—
> Branching, veined, barked,
> The fine black hairs
> That need sunlight to be seen,
> Lines, branches, the universal M,
> Cain's mark.
>
> Raise your hand, hold it,
> Know the stilling of winter,
> And when you grow tired, forget
> And let it fall, the flow
> Of new springs.
>
> You rub your eyes,
> Bone, skin on water,

You see heavens, stars,
Fires, fire.

Leaves riddle with sunlight
The ground, the grass,
Your hand, holding sunlight,
Leaves of shadow, of air.

This is to say that both kinds of knowing, literature and science, are vehicles that carry us out of our solipsistic selves and into the world. Both make it possible for us to recognize one another as real beings moving in a real world. I tried to say something like this in a poem in which I imagined the world as it might have been viewed by the first woman to orbit the earth, in 1963, Lt. Col. Valentina Vladimirovna Tereshkova. The poem itself makes an orbit, closing in a circle, and pulls lines from Genesis and Job into its scientific compass. (I should mention that the Daugava is a river in Latvia, one of the Baltic countries whose rightfully independent status has now been recognized. That the Daugava, in this poem, is "tangy" is an allusion to—what else?—Tang, fabled orange drink of space missions!)

It looked like an apple
or a Christmas orange:
I wanted to eat it.
I could taste the juice
trickling down my throat,
my tongue smarted,
my teeth were chilled.
How sweet those mountains seemed,
how cool and tangy, the Daugava!

What scrawl of history
had sent me so far from home? . . .

When I was a girl in school, comrades,
seemingly lazy as a lizard
sprawled on a rock in Tashkent,
I dreamed of conquest.

My hands tugged at my arms,
I caught flies on my tongue.

Now my soul's as hushed as the Steppes on a winter night;
snow drifts in my brain, something
shifts, sinks, subsides inside,

and some undying pulse hoists my body
like a flag, and sends me up,
like Nureyev.
From my samovar I fill my cup with air,
and it overflows.
Who knows who scatters the bright cloud?

Two days and almost twenty-three hours
I looked at light,
scanning its lines like a book.

My conclusions:

At last I saw the way
time turns,
like a key in a lock,
and night becomes day,
and sun burns away the primeval mist,
and day is, and is not.

Listen, earthmen,
comrades of the soil,
I saw the Black Sea shrink to a drop
of dew and disappear;
I could blot out Mother Russia with my thumb in thin air;
the whole world was nearly not there.

It looked like an apple
or a Christmas orange:
I wanted to eat it.
I thought, It is pleasant to the eyes,
good for food,
and eating it would make men and women wise.

I could taste the juice
trickling down my throat,
my tongue smarted,
my teeth were chilled.
How sweet those mountains seemed,
how cool and tangy, the Daugava!

The Scottish poet Hugh MacDiarmid, in his essay "Poetry and Science," his own response to C. P. Snow's call for communication between scientists and artists, nicely quoted Chekhov, pledging allegiance to Chekhov's stated goal: "Familiarity with the natural sciences and with scientific methods has always kept me on my guard, and I have always tried, where it was possible, to be consistent with the facts of science." We do not want to fail to speak, or hear, any of those voices crying "I am" in the wilderness of our existence.

Many years have passed since C. P. Snow made his plea for communication between scientists and nonscientists. There are some things time has shown he was wrong about. He did not foresee the ways in which the literary canon would be stretched or revised. He did not foresee that the Soviet Union could ever be faced with economic calamity, with the result that what was left of it would wind up putting its space program up for sale to any and all buyers. He did not foresee that the "scientific revolution," which he said had followed on the industrial revolution, would be succeeded by what people are calling "the information revolution." I am sure he did not foresee that I would write this essay on a computer.

He did not foresee poets like Robert Watson and Al Zolynas, or many others, or numerous writers who would pursue an understanding of the scientific world in creative prose.

But his thesis, that scientists and nonscientists need to try to understand each other's language, is as generally valid as ever. When cultures meet, the first order of business is translation. This is as true for cultures of knowledge as for cultures of race or gender or nationality. *If we cannot even speak to one another, what good does it do us to have something to say?*

And if we speak only to ourselves, how long will we have anything new to say? We must listen to one another, if we are not to grow old telling the same anecdotes over and over, mumbling our way into graves of habit.

It is rather like two cultures meeting, then, this interchange between scientist and poet. It is rather like conversation and friendship. It is rather like strolling hand-in-hand across a shining suspension bridge flung over the endless drop into our own unknowing. Finally, here at the end of the twentieth century, it must be, for all our sakes, rather like scientist and poet accompanying each other into the twenty-first.

Dancing to the Beat of Her Heart

I WAS NEVER ANY GOOD AT POP CULTURE, but that doesn't mean I didn't try to be. There was a tavern at the end of the road, and after school let out and before dinner, high school kids were allowed in to dance. The rumor was that if a scout spotted you you would get to be on Dick Clark's *American Bandstand*. You would be on television, a thought that thrilled me although I had never seen a television except in newspaper advertisements. I had a circle skirt—two circle skirts. One was made of felt; the other was a blue-and-white dotted Swiss that I had made myself in Home Ec, sewing the heart-shaped pocket by hand. I wore a white sleeveless blouse with a V-neck. Under my circle skirt I had crinolines, stiff and flirty. But all this sophistication was nothing compared with the black-and-white saddle shoes and rolled white socks.

My sister, younger by two and a half years, observed my shenanigans on the dance floor with disapproval. On the way home she said, "I was so embarrassed! I was so ashamed! You're not supposed to move your hips like that when you dance!"

I tried a very few more times in my life to learn to dance. The bop, the twist, the two-step. I never got the hang of any of them. Besides, when I was seventeen, and briefly one of just thirteen female students attending New Mexico Tech, a guy who had actually said he loved me hauled off and slapped me on a dance floor. He was twenty-four, a graduate student in physics. I can't remember what it was I had done wrong—a twirl, a step, a glide. Maybe it didn't have anything to do with dancing.

My course load that semester included calculus, physics, analytic geometry, anthropology, mechanical drawing, something else I've forgotten. On my own, I read *Dr. Zhivago*, a dry, piney wind sweeping sand through the dormitory, which resembled a bunker. Home was far away; my parents said it would be silly—a waste of money—to go back for Thanksgiving or even Christmas. On Christmas Day, I did calculus problems from seven in the morning until ten at night. (Those are the exact hours. I wanted to see if I could keep doing problems without stopping.) Some nights I went walking by myself in the gulch, the moon as bright as a flashlight. I didn't go to any more dances.

There were car rides, though, flying fast over long stretches of deserted southwestern highway. For a semester.

After that I adopted a bystander's relation to pop culture. For a while, there were Janis Joplin, the Grateful Dead, Jefferson Airplane. Microminis superseded by maxicoats superseded by power suits. Fishnet stockings followed by thigh-high kick-ass boots followed by pumps-for-professionals followed by Nikes. (I await the return of saddle shoes.) Fashion is everywhere. What is the pop culture of American politics but fashion? What is the pop culture of contemporary fiction but fashion? In time, a woman settles down. Perhaps she lives alone. Perhaps no one asks her to dance, but an American woman, even a bystander, even a wallflower, lives in a pop world. Fashion *is* everywhere. Lately, lately, I pop—pop!—popcorn and watch the Academy Awards on television. I read *People* magazine. I even read *Vanity Fair*, which is top-of-the-pop pop, pure promo, la crème de la puff.

And sometimes I remember what it was like, riding in a car, the windows down, the radio on . . .

I don't think my sister remembers what she said. I would never bring it up to her. She could never have guessed that I would be foolish enough to take her childish words so seriously . . .

To be loved, I think, would be like being included, made a part of that chic clique, the human race. Women are always promising to be true. If a woman were loved in return, I think, she would feel like she was in an automobile, riding along, with somebody beside her because that's where he wanted to be. She would be tapping her foot in time to the beat. She would be dancing to the beat of her heart.

Meaning and Music in
George Garrett's Fiction

> I have come to believe—indeed I have to believe it insofar as I believe
> in the validity and efficacy of art—that what comes to us first and
> foremost through the body, as a sensuous affective experience, is taken
> and transformed by mind and self into a thing of the spirit.
>
> —George Garrett, "My Two One-Eyed Coaches"

WHAT WE LACK IN MUCH CONTEMPORARY FICTION is music—the long
line, the grace note, the dance of clauses, and especially, the whole
idea of a sustained development, invention succeeding invention with
logic and intensity and creating a *world* of intrareferences that define
and connect, unite and separate, the finished work a planetary body,
as it were, loosed from its creator, held in place by gravity, held aloft
by levity, and moving in harmony with the spheres.

What we get in much contemporary fiction is MTV—short scenes,
stylization, self-consciousness. This is fiction that is clumsy, earth-
bound, flat-footed. It is not a world but a perspective; it is a *take*—a
single view of a single thing. It has no music beyond the single voice
of its creator, because music takes place in time, and this fiction does
not: it is afraid of time, it wants to defeat time. (Or perhaps, since
many of its creators are young, it does not yet know that time exists.)

Whereas the fiction of George Garrett, for example, projects itself
into time, as if time is a kind of space.

What we are employing here is, of course, the powerful metaphor
of incarnation. To assume a body and by means of it penetrate time

is an act of love—it can't be performed by someone who is afraid or unaware of time.

But without that movement into time, that willingness to inhabit a space that is not oneself, that being-unafraid-to-enter a space not oneself and inhabit it without constantly worrying whether you will be able to return to yourself (because if you do, you will *not* perform, you will never escape from the ever-present consciousness of yourself), there is no music.

In an interview, George Garrett said, "There is a *conversation* that goes on in an unbroken way between the reader and the writer. . . . There's . . . a real copulative spirit going in the reading experience."

Thinking this over in his essential book *Understanding George Garrett*, R. H. W. Dillard argues that for Garrett "[t]he writer's obligation is to establish that 'copulative spirit,' to enlist the reader in the creation of the text." Indeed, Dillard says, "Any understanding of his later work, and particularly *The Magic Striptease, The Succession*, and *Poison Pen*, depends heavily on an awareness of Garrett's determination to 'produce a new reader' capable of sharing actively in that significant conversation with the properly generative 'copulative spirit.' "

But how has George Garrett gone about trying to "produce a new reader"? After all, all of us who write desire an interaction with our reader. We writers are such horny little bastards, eager to love and be loved—has George Garrett *really* found a new way to woo the reader?

I think he has. With music. A music I will try to explain by excerpt and account for by biography (but we haven't an adequate vocabulary, in our critical tradition, for a full discussion of music in fictional prose).

I remember the night I heard Garrett read from *The Succession*, his extraordinary novel, set in Elizabethan England, about the creation and perception of history. I held my breath, not wanting even the sound of my own breathing to intrude on the glorious music of his sentences. But it is interesting to observe that these sentences are not regularly Ciceronian periods—not oratory, not even (often) the biblical rhetoric that informs so much Southern fiction, and even a fair amount of his own early fiction. He had found a way—or rather, had decided to pursue a way that had appeared here and there in the earlier work—of making a long line *out of smaller lines*. Look at this moment, chosen at random, from that book (the reader is being told that Queen Elizabeth knows of Sir Robert Cecil's illicit correspondence with James IV of Scotland, destined to be King James of England):

> She will hear him out on any subject whatsoever. But without truly listening to him. Certainly without truly believing him. For she knows that his heart and mind are chiefly elsewhere. Are uneasy in attendance in Scotland. For a fact. Heart and mind secretly in service of that man he takes to be most likely to be the King when she is gone.

This is a sequence of, mostly, sentence fragments (bane of writing teachers!), but the fragments have been pieced together in such a way as to create the overall illusion of a single sentence—and yet the full stops heighten the rises and deepen the falls within the confines of the "sentence." The dynamic range, so to speak, is far greater than it would be if the full stops were muted to commas or semicolons, the forward high-note thrust of the capitals pulled back to the more modest upright stance of the lowercase. It is as if the sentence contained several voices, a chorus of voices, some pitched higher and some lower, some louder and some softer, and though of course a sentence is not a chorus and we cannot hear its voices all at once, the way we hear voices in a chorus, we feel as though we somehow very nearly can, because in addition to the melodious rise and fall produced by the sentence fragmentation, we hear a fugal interplay among the fragments, and it is this which keeps the fragmentation from becoming merely mannerist and tiresome, as it otherwise might.

Note how "For" echoes "For," how "heart and mind" quickly becomes a motif, repeated. Note how the fragments are *different* fragments, some beginning with a conjunction, another with an adverb, another with a verb, another with a preposition, and the last with a noun, so that there is a general effect of overlapping and connecting but also of advancing, one part an echo or a shadow of another, the next a foreshadow or herald of what is to follow. Imagine a single sentence:

> She will hear him out on any subject whatsoever, but without truly listening to him, and certainly without truly believing him, for she knows that his heart and mind are chiefly elsewhere, in Scotland, secretly in service, however uneasily, of that man he takes to be most likely to be the King when she is gone.

This sentence is not bad—for starters, it *exists*, and in much contemporary fiction, it would not, it would have been consigned to the margin—but if it is more complex than the sentences to be found in that other contemporary fiction, it is a great deal less complex than what Garrett has done with it. Composed of units of varying lengths and syntactical formation, given range and harmonic volume by the quality of echo, made mysterious by the sense of shadow as if there were peaks and valleys in the jagged cascade of fragments, simultaneously haunted by the past (the first fragment brought motivically forward) and eagerly pushing forward into the future (the ongoing narrative drive toward sense), Garrett's "sentence" (for this reader, at any rate) is a siren song.

To divide a sentence into syntactical units and scramble and repeat certain of the units or parts of the units while moving forward toward the sense of the whole is not the only way to make music in literature, but it is an interesting and distinctive way. And it is one way of accomplishing in prose the brilliant thing that Beethoven did in music: to build his architectonic musical structures, my father liked to point out, Beethoven used relatively small units. So many writers (or composers, or painters) think that the way to make an aesthetically large statement is to *start* with something big—but that is the way to create a structure that will almost certainly collapse in the middle (the middle being always the point, in any work of art, of greatest structural stress). One must start with something small, and add to that small thing something else small, and add to *that* another small thing—and this is the way to devise size.

(You have to be smart enough, strong enough, and tenacious enough to put *enough* small things together. You have to be able to figure out which small thing can go with which other small thing. They should be worthwhile small things.)

For a writer, these "small things" need not be sentence fragments, but Garrett, increasingly, does choose sentence fragments to work with, placing them in such lovely, complicated relation to one another that their rise and fall, their dynamics and wide diapason, leave the reader breathless.

He does not do this only in *The Succession* or even only in fiction. In nonfiction as straightforward as the essay "My Two One-Eyed Coaches," a tribute to two teachers, the reader encounters the same technique right at the beginning:

> I came to reading and writing more or less naturally. As, for example, you might come to swimming early and easily. Which, matter of fact, I did; learning to swim at about the same time I learned to walk. I can very well remember the name of the man (he was the swimming coach at Rollins College near Orlando, where I grew up during the Depression years) who took me as a toddler and threw me off the end of a dock into a deep lake where I had the existential choice of sinking or swimming. And chose to swim, thank you very much.

As I say, this technique leaves the reader breathless with admiration—but it also leaves the reader breathless with *exertion*. The essay touches on the delights and difficulties of a number of athletic activities, but central to it, as to Garrett's life, is the sport of boxing. Well, then, consider that the writer throws himself into his sentence —and then pulls back from it, feints, considers another approach, does some fancy footwork, jabs at the air, pulls his punches, and when you least expect it, lands a punch square on the jaw or in the stomach. The reader reels.

In the essay, Garrett talks about what he learned from athletic coaches: "conditioning" (the art of preparation) and "concentration" (the art of execution) and "compensation" (the art of art). Boxing, he learned that "[t]o hit the other guy you had to move in close enough for him to hit you. No other way." It strikes me that Garrett's syntax has that same sense of intimacy and risk. He is so physically *present* in his prose that the reader is placed on his toes, must pay attention. The reader finds *himself* dancing around the ring, on the lookout— until what had appeared almost pugnaciously aggressive is seen to be, in the clinches, an embrace, a desire to be paid attention *to*, a willingness to risk exposure.

To expand on the difference between his fiction and much contemporary fiction: If much contemporary fiction is MTV, the reader in relation to it is obliged to be a couch potato. Garrett's work, in contrast, actually requires of the reader a response.

And this is how, I would like to suggest, Garrett establishes that "copulative spirit" between author and reader that generates the text. Having lured the reader by the siren song of his sentence, he engages the reader in a syntactical sportiveness that leads, as all encounters do (our mothers warned us), to what comes next. Which is, that is, that movement into time of which we were speaking. I have no doubt that for an author with so ardent a love of language, it may be, it will be, that the best reader of all will be time herself.

With Susan Sontag in Illinois

SUSAN SONTAG HATES TELEVISION. She said this at a party in Illinois. She was sitting on a couch, drinking rum and smoking a cigarette, the white streak, in her dark hair, like something bright and fast, a shooting star, a comet.

College administrators and faculty and a few handpicked students made a polite effort to talk with one another, but the person we all wanted to hear was Susan Sontag and conversation faltered and halted as we turned our attention in her direction. There was pasta primavera on my plate, which I balanced on my knees.

As soon as I got back to my motel—for all parties end, and when they do, women writers on literary tour find themselves back in their motel rooms, and each woman writer's motel room will be furnished with one bed, one dressing table, and one very large, swivel-mounted television set—I turned on the TV.

Before I remembered what Susan Sontag had said, I turned it on. She had said television is a drug, an addiction. *You can't help yourself,* she might have been saying to me now, fiery, and flicking cigarette ash; *admit that you are powerless in the grip of your habit.*

But television is my life! I would cry out. And so it is: television is my social life. Parties with Susan Sontag are, let's face it, rare, at least for me. More often, I spend my Saturday nights with the Golden Girls, where I get to be the baby of the bunch. Mary Tyler Moore was one of my best friends when I was a struggling career girl, and Murphy Brown, managing without a man, is just doing what I do—granted that I do it on less pay and without designer suits, and granted that I'm not carrying a child out of wedlock and so have been spared Dan Quayle's opprobrium. Am I going to fault Murphy Brown for her *family values?* Am I going to stand in front of the mirror and point an accusatory finger at myself? Excuse me, but I did that for years. This country is short on good men, which is no reason to blame the women.

It's true that television is mostly terrible. What isn't? Broadway? The best-seller list?

Besides, I like a little reductionism now and then. Life is hard. I mean, it is really, really *hard*, and great art helps us to know how hard, but great art also makes the knowledge bearable. When great art fails to be present, we need to fudge our knowing, too. This is what sitcoms are all about. It may even be what best-sellers are all about.

So I am all for Murphy Brown. It was April in Illinois, but I could hardly wait for Murphy to return for the fall season. I wanted to welcome her back. If I couldn't bring her up to date on the news in my life, I wanted to find out what was going on in hers. My dog, Duncan, and I would curl up on the bed and tune in. Would she stay single after she had her baby? Would she keep working? Would her baby be colicky, a miniature Murphy?

Of course, I remind myself a few months later, Murphy Brown is only a television character. I know that. But the thing about addiction is that it takes over your whole life; you begin to equate all of life with the thing you are addicted to. You mistake it for real life. You mistake it for, say, Dan Quayle. But hey, that channel's been changed!

On the sunny midwestern morning following that party, Sontag was scheduled to speak about metaphor, but mostly she told us of her childhood reading habits and her current theatrical productions in Europe. These were both interesting things to hear about; still, their intrusion on the ostensible subject brought to my mind the way celebrity is always intruding on writing, at least here, in America. It is as if we are all in a gigantic sitcom, the American Celebrity-Culture Sitcom, this show where we all sit around watching ourselves. *This show that fudges our knowledge—for we do possess the knowledge, and it possesses us, deny it as we will—of how hard everything really is.* On a cherry-wood sideboard there were fresh orange juice and hot coffee and sweet rolls for all, and Sontag talked about herself, which was, as I say, interesting, and if it was not easy to tell where the commercial breaks began and ended, that, too, is what our contemporary American literature—I don't say Sontag's, which encompasses some excellent essays, or any author's in particular; I'm not going to point an accusatory finger at anybody—is, often, about.

Letter from the Philippines

CROSSING A STREET IN MANILA

THE CREATIVE WRITING STUDENTS in the small seminar room at Ateneo University in Metro Manila were answering my question about the relation of language to politics in the Philippines. With that youthful energy that is each generation's greatest natural resource they talked about the "feudal system" Filipinos have lived under, about the centrality of village life, about the Filipino's innately "romantic" soul and love of theater. The electric power had gone off—brownouts were lasting up to seven hours a day—and, in late May, the room's temperature quickly soared. Just as suddenly, a rainstorm rushed across the sky, as if in a hurry to get somewhere else; afterwards, flame trees and acacias seemed to lean in the direction it had gone, like lovers left behind at a train station.

I was explaining to the class that anything might be the subject of a short-short. "A door," I said, pointing at the door through which we had entered. "Or a table." I touched the table around which we were grouped. "This morning," I admitted, "it occurred to me that one might write a short-short about crossing a street in Manila."

The students laughed. "That's not a short-short," one said; "that's a novel! A saga! An *epic*, at least!"

Because of the brownouts, traffic lights often did not work. Sometimes there were police to direct the flow of traffic, and sometimes there were not. That morning I had been making my way with a

133

group of faculty women from St. Scholastica's College to a fast-food Chinese restaurant. I have traveled a lot and have never met a warmer, friendlier, more welcoming people than Filipinos. A good thing, too, I thought, as I imagined, marooned there on the traffic island, that I might have to give up all hope of returning home. I would marry, become a citizen and cast my defiant but losing vote for Miriam Santiago, and grow old on my own little "island" among the more than seven thousand that make up the archipelago that is the Philippines. All around me were trucks, cars, taxicabs, jeepneys, tricycles, and pedicabs. Pedicabs are bicycles with sidecars; tricycles are motorcycles with sidecars; jeepneys, ostensibly another method of public transportation, are a mobile art form. This really is re-*cycling*. Jeeps left over from World War II are painted in elaborate, colorful detail, outfitted with model horses, dressed in flags and pennants, draped with purple curtains, and named. *Banana Magnet*, said one. *Desert*, said another, as if it were the punch line to a running, or rolling, joke. *Last Waltz* was the mournful title of a third. Then there was the jeepney that demanded, apocalyptically, *Saint or Sinner:* I felt put on the spot.

At St. Scholastica's I had read a paper on the short fiction of women in the United States today. Everywhere I went, I met Filipino writers and scholars who were not only acquainted with the work of American writers—they were frequently acquainted with the writers themselves. A number had been to the International Writing Workshop in Iowa City. Ed and Edith Tiempo recalled being in Paul Engle's class alongside the now late Flannery O'Connor. Mimeographing was expensive back then, Edith Tiempo said, so the students read their stories aloud in class. But they had to ask Engle to read O'Connor's stories for her, because no one could understand that Georgia accent. "She had an annoying habit of twisting a lock of hair at her forehead," Edith said, laughing softly, adding that when Engle found unconvincing a sex scene O'Connor had written the author responded, "Come out to my car and I'll show you how it's done."

I loved these stories and scribbled them down in my spiral notebook at night in my wonderful room in The Manila Hotel, where the

MacArthur Suite can be booked for $1,400 a day and often is—by the Japanese, who, presumably, think $1,400 a day is not too much to pay for the right to report to their friends that they have slept in the MacArthur Suite! From my more modest room I could look out at Manila Bay with its twinkling cargo ships, the world coming and going and always bigger than I'd dreamed. It is stories like this that link us, make us members of a larger literary community. Gossip makes us real to one another.

Another writer, F. Sionil José, prolific and outspoken, whose *Three Filipino Women* was being published in the United States by Random House, explained to me that Melville and Emerson are the American writers who are "relevant" to him, because they had made an *American* tradition, "throwing off the colonial influence." He likes the contemporary black writers for the same reason.

Weaving—amazingly—among the cars had been adults and children selling single sticks of gum, cigarettes, anything. A boy tapped on a window and opened his palm, begging. No doubt he lived, if he had any address at all, in the poor-beyond-saying Tondo district. I could say how seeing him made me feel, but I can't say how he felt. The Filipino writers will have to tell us that. Every country finds its own words. And out of those words it constructs an idea of itself. Literature, also, makes us real to one another.

At the University of the Philippines, the splendidly lively National Artist Francisco Arcellana ("That means I get to be buried for free") pointed out that deconstructionist theory comes from the French— "an overrefined culture," he said nicely.

To be in search of a language with which to define one's sense of oneself, one's entire country—how exciting! And here in the West we are so eager to discard what we know that we turn a deaf ear even to our own words, eliminating the text, the author, the authoritative voice. I began to understand the lure of the East, the temptation to believe in something besides criticism.

Arcellana was inducting students into the UP Writing Club. He made them raise their right hands. "I promise to write, *write*, WRITE," he had them repeat after him. "And never be silenced!"

On my traffic island I had been clutching a light canvas bag a former student had made for me. She had had my name printed on one side, and the cover art from one of my novels on the other, and I used the bag to carry the books I would be giving readings from. I was also carrying my paper on women writers. And I was also carrying a Sportsac bag that held my money and passport and traveling cosmetics and sunglasses and sunscreen. I had been clutching this stuff and standing there, in the middle of a street in Manila, and waiting for traffic to slacken, and these are some of the thoughts I was thinking.

Why did the writer cross the road? It was never simply to get to the other side.

A Brief Encounter with Faulkner

IN A NOW-FAMOUS INTERVIEW, Faulkner said that one good poem—his example was the "Ode on a Grecian Urn"—was worth any number of little old ladies. "The writer's only responsibility," he said, "is to his art. He will be completely ruthless if he is a good one."

I cannot swear that Faulkner was serious; I do know that any number of beginning writers have taken him at his word and have thereby been led to assume a separation of art from reality as dire in its consequences as the Cartesian dichotomy between mind and body.

Imagine for a moment a world full of poems, a world in which, however, not one little old lady exists.

I, for one, wish that it were not so easy to imagine such a world, but it is easy, at least for me, because, as I write this, my own mother is dying, slowly and surely. She is dying, and she is a little old lady.

Should I say then that I would give all the poems in the world could I keep my mother here? Sometimes I think I would say that—and then I hear with my inner ear that poetry of sound to which *she* gave her life. She played the violin. It was her life.

For the way of things, here on earth, is that a little old lady will lose her life whether writers are ruthless or kind. (And her husband, whose life too, though he forgets more of it with every passing day, was playing the violin, will lose his. And dogs die like dogs, no matter how many Nobel prizes are handed out to writers. And no matter how much we love anyone or anything, parents or dogs or even writing.)

Furthermore, to swap poems for little old ladies, like swapping little old ladies for poems, would be to beg one of the most important questions any writer must answer: What is the relation between little old ladies and poetry? What is the relation between literature and reality, between art and reality?

It is like—as I said above—the relation between body and mind. Each—body, mind—is, in this world at any rate, essential for the other's full existence.

My mother, even dying, knows that. Did Faulkner?

Faulkner was wily; he protected himself from intrusions, and interviewers, the better to observe the real world, the world of reality, around him. Did this real world include little old ladies? Well, whether or not he ever observed little old ladies, I *can* swear he certainly had an eye for young girls. Once, when I was still a student of philosophy in Charlottesville, Virginia, I passed him on the sidewalk in front of Mincer's Pipe Shop. He was wearing his Tyrolean hat.

I am ashamed to say that at first I didn't even see him—to me, at twenty, an old man—because I was busy thinking about art. A friend I was with told me to turn around fast, if I wanted to see Faulkner. I turned around, fast, and there he was. *Faulkner.* Our eyes met, Faulkner's and mine, because Faulkner had for some reason turned around to look back at me.

And I was not even wearing a Tyrolean hat.

The Place Where There Is Writing

THE NAME OF THE PLACE IS DZIBILCHALTÚN, or, translated from the Mayan, "the place where there is writing." Sometimes the translation is extended to "the place where there is writing on flat rocks." The rocks, or stelae, are gone. Perhaps they are in a museum, with the other Mayan hieroglyphics, or buried still in this vast archaeological zone that remains mostly unexplored. I didn't look for them the way a historian might have; I am not a historian. What I cared about was the eeriness of the place, and its implicative name, as layered with meaning as Troy with time.

I had been in Mérida, the capital of Yucatán and thirteen miles south of Dzibilchaltún, only a day and a half. I'd suffered a head wound just before leaving the States, and although the wound was slight, the bandage plastered to the back of my head was impressive. Because I keeled over every time I tried to stand up, and because the bandage loudly said why, the flight attendants had bundled me in blankets—in August—and wheelchaired me through the Atlanta and Mérida airports.

But now I felt better, and I'd taken the bandage off, found the foreign exchange bank, and hopped a second-class bus to Dzibilchaltún. Dzibilchaltún is not a site most tourists visit; it tends to be overwhelmed by the more fully excavated and therefore more immediately exotic ruins at, for example, Uxmal, Kabáh, Chichén Itzá, Cobá, and Tulum. It was my good luck, as it turned out, to have undergone my mild physical shock. I was obliged to begin by staying close to home

139

base. And so I went to a place many miss—the place where there is writing.

Home base was a *posada*, an inn, in Mérida. It was near the busy *zócalo*, or town square, a pretty square with stone love seats for courting couples, and box yews surrounding benches where old men and women, their courtship days behind them, sat and talked while their grandchildren played. The bus station was on the other side of the *zócalo*.

As the bus pulled out of the city, past double-parked cars, the marketplace, furniture stores, and computer centers, we moved back in time. It happened with a startling swiftness. Mayan cottages, one-room mortared stone dwellings with flat, thatched roofs, lined the highway. Men worked on the highway, cutting back the jungle that would overtake it in three months if they didn't—if they simply, one day, fed up and worn out, called it quits, stuck their machetes and picks back in their trucks, and went home to lie down in their hammocks. They don't go home; they hack away at that jungle every day. The kids mill around the houses, at the edge of the highway, and shout, *"Un peso, un peso"*; they'll pose for a picture. They learn early to squeeze what spare change they can out of sentimental tourists.

I was the only tourist on this particular bus, though. There were few other passengers of any stripe. We were not traveling anybody's usual route at the usual time of day, although at other times there are Mexicans and Indians coming into Mérida or going home from work. It was noon. Some grownups lolled around the roadside houses with the kids. To the unwitting tourist, they might look as if they were too lazy to work, but they'd been up working in the fields since 4 or 5 A.M. They'd already put in a full day of backbreaking labor. They would take their siesta, these who'd found a few free moments in a seemingly endless workday, and then put in more hours, crafting gewgaws for the tourist market, weaving hammocks—anything to earn a living, to get by.

There are often nine to fifteen children in these Indian families. They speak Mayan among themselves, but we have forgotten how to write it. The kids play in the dirt, surrounded by the chickens that run loose in the yards. An occasional horse stands stolidly nearby, flicking its tail at flies. Underwear drips from clotheslines, or dries flat, spread out on low bushes.

The breeze the bus's motion made blew in through the open window, welcome on my face. We passed pepper trees, banana trees, hibiscus, a gap-toothed stone fence filled in with a tire and some string, fences made of piled stone, unmortared, with vines growing in and out of the spaces between the stones, and a chapel with a faded mint-green front, three open arches at the top through which blue sky was framed, with a small cross atop each of two of the arches and the third cross missing. I wondered what had happened to the third cross.

The fields along this route, as in much of Yucatán, were planted in henequen—what we call sisal. The henequen plant has wide, tough, rigid leaves; its fibers are strong. I have a sisal rug in my living room in Wisconsin; I bought it because it was cheaper than a "real" rug. Now when I walk across that rug, I know who paid for it.

Platoons of field workers passed us, going the opposite way, toward Mérida; they leant against the sides of the open backs of their trucks; they were going home, to the look-alike subdivisions on the city's outskirts. The sun was hot; it was, as I say, August. "The wrong time of year to visit Yucatán." I went when I could.

The driver let me off in what appeared to be the middle of nowhere, pointing at a dirt road. I followed his finger; the bus left. I was alone. The absence of anyone made me feel as though someone must be there somewhere, lurking behind the squat trees. But if I turned back, I'd have to wait five hours for the bus to make its return journey. The heat stung; mosquitoes were biting. I tilted my straw hat to keep my face in shade, rubbed suntan oil over my bare arms. After a while, people appeared in the road ahead of me. A Mexican family. A Latino couple, lovers. They had come in cars.

There's an admission stand with a ticket to buy, the omnipresent and necessary soft drinks in a lift-top cooler, and, as you might guess, more children eager to have their pictures taken—for *un peso*. A small girl volunteered to serve as a guide to the one-room museum. Since I knew no Spanish, and she knew no English, and the museum's careful explanations of the exhibition bore no subtitles, I hadn't, for the most part, any idea what I was viewing. But my guide chattered away as if none of this mattered. Maybe it didn't; I knew from my travel book that the seven figurines at which I stared had been taken from the temple I was going to see, and that they were singular in type. None like them has ever been found elsewhere in that part of the world. Each of these figurines is hideously deformed. Historians conjecture that they were used in medical rites, to cure like conditions. They gave me the willies. And, as I say, I'm no historian, so I posed my little guide in another part of the museum, snapped her picture, and reached into my pocket for change. She didn't know that what I was really buying was her smile, a wonderful, shy smile that had to sit on itself not to become a grin. She danced around me, my very own Munchkin, as I set off down the road once more.

Now there were plenty of people, natives, but they were headed for the swimming pool. The pool, of course, is a *cenote*, a well, thought to be the deepest in Yucatán. There are bones at the bottom, some of them elongated, pointed skulls that were shaped by boards pressed in a certain configuration on the malleable heads of newborn, upper-class infants. This is one of the wells that the Mayans used for human sacrifice. Yucatán officialdom likes to blame the practice of human sacrifice on the Toltecs, a much-later, conquering civilization; the Mayans, they emphasize, were a cultured people, advanced in astronomy and agriculture, living by a complex calendar, rich in art, honoring mind and body, sport and scholarship. This is true, as the most casual tourist can see. The vaguest acquaintance with the mathematics of the Mayan calendar and its adhibitions in politics, art and science, and religion will bowl anyone over. Nevertheless, not all ancient Mayans shared in the benefits of their culture; the societal structure plainly was stratified and elitist. As for human sacrifice, the offering of live bodies, said to have been drugged beforehand, to the rain god Chac, there is evidence enough that the Mayans practiced it long before the Toltec invasion. Evidence is here, in the *cenote* at Dzibilchaltún. The site at Dzibilchaltún goes back at least to 600 B.C., when it may have been an outpost or advance settlement of the Mayans then primarily located on the other side of Mexico, along the Pacific, and by still-conservative estimate, it has been dated to

1000 B.C.; many researchers date its beginning hundreds of years earlier. At any rate, it is believed to be the oldest continuously occupied Mayan city-state. It may have flourished before Homer lived; it may be that Troy has nothing on Dzibilchaltún.

Still, these facts—if, given our incomplete state of knowledge, they can be called facts—can be easily looked up or pieced together by anyone who is interested in them; I've nothing new to bring to them, and so, though I am someone who is interested, I set them aside to continue my walk.

From the pool came sounds of splashing—and, yes, transistor radios and portable television sets. I crawled around the Spanish chapel, built in 1590 to "Christianize" the heathen spirit that may have lingered in the surrounding area, hiding behind rocks, swimming far below the surface of the *cenote*.

There were rocks everywhere, strewn haphazardly as if they'd been a manuscript some author, in a fit of pique, had torn lengthwise and crosswise and tossed to the wind. I followed the turn in the path that led to the Mayan arch. The arch marks the start of the *sacbe*, the ceremonial way to another city-state. I was headed for the one standing Mayan structure here, among an untellable number that once existed; it has been partially reconstructed. It is the Temple of the Seven Dolls.

The Latino lovers walked in front of me; I could see people at the temple, but they were walking away from it, back toward the direction I had come from. A storm was kicking up. Only the lovers and I were walking toward the temple. The path we walked is sometimes called the Road of the Gods. The blue sky had darkened; rain clouds were gathering in the distance, like tribes coming together. Nearer to hand, a great loneliness seemed to sweep over the fallen stones.

Octavio Paz, in an essay titled "The Seed" in *Alternating Current*, tries to describe "[a] time before the idea of antiquity: the real original time." Finding he can reach for it only metaphorically, he calls it "the original metaphor," and writes that

> it is the imminence of the unknown—not as a presence but as an expectation and a threat, as an emptiness. It is the breaking through

of the *now* into the *here*, the present in all its instantaneous actuality and all its dizzying, hostile potentiality. What is this moment concealing?

I sensed that presence. I knew the moment was concealing something—but what?

Paz, trapped into describing "the original metaphor" metaphorically, tries again: He calls it "the seed," the future contained—or concealed—in the present. He says that

> the calendar clears a path through the dense thickets of time, makes its immense expanse navigable. . . . *[N]ow* falls into *before* and *after*. This fissure in time announces the advent of the kingdom of man.

I have long held that the Fall was a fall into Time, and that there is no time without language. The Fall was a fall into Language. In the beginning was the Word, but we learned to say "I," and that prideful self-assertion was the original sin. It was also the beginning of language. It is not consciousness but self-consciousness, which allows us to see ourselves as subjects, and to see ourselves as objects of our subjective seeing, and so on as in an endless series of mirrors, that separates us from God. That separates us, period. The ability to refer to ourselves grants us history and hope, the foreknowledge of our death and legacy, the knowledge, to put it in other words, of good and evil. For with the reflexive recognition of ourselves as subjects that are their own objects comes the inescapable awareness of cause and consequence. Without language there would be no morality, only perfection; with language comes knowledge. It is a small matter, at this point, whether that knowledge is perceived, construed, imagined, provable or unprovable. It is a very large matter that our capacity to know that we know is a function of language. The original sin was the original metaphor. The original metaphor was the original sin. It goes without saying that this is a guilt of which no writer, especially, would wish to be absolved. The writer prays, Save me, O Lord, but not yet; I have books to write first.

I may not be a historian, but I am, I confess, a writer, and I'll go anywhere where there is writing. I climbed the steps to the top of the temple. It was open on all four sides; the lovers sat on the steps on the opposite side.

The sky had become completely overcast. Rain clouds had dropped closer to the ground. The wind that had come up as I walked was now gusting; it wore an expression of ferocity; it tunneled through the doorways and windows of the temple as if through a wind tunnel; it blew my hair in my face and made a sound like someone blowing through a hollow reed, a mournful sound with an undernote of the kind of despair that leads to a desire for revenge. The lovers had brought their lunch to make a picnic; I opened the plastic bag of trail mix I'd been given by a new acquaintance at the *posada*.

The sky was black now. I could see rain in the distance, across miles of scrub brush. Thunder pitched toward the temple as if it were being thrown at me. The wind was so strong I had to put the trail mix away before it got blown away. The lovers had packed up their picnic, raised an umbrella, and run off down the dirt road. I was alone in the Mayan ruin.

There was a famous, but unfortunately forgetful, archaeologist who was killed by lightning when he took shelter at the top of another Mayan structure during another storm. He should have known better. I had no reason to know any better. I didn't know these heights draw lightning or that I might well be killed. I stood fascinated in the ruins, letting the wind snarl my hair, watching the lightning tear at the sky, and watching the rain fall first here, then there. I was alone in the Mayan ruin with the rain god Chac.

Rain spattered the rocks; the rocks turned dark with the wet. It was as if Chac were writing on them. We were alone there, Chac and I, and I felt that if I only knew how to read Mayan, I could read rain on rock. What is this moment *revealing?*

I sighed, knowing that I did not know.

Suddenly the rain ceased. The wind fled the temple. I scanned the site. The clouds had crossed overhead and disappeared into the horizon. The sun reclaimed its territory, and the green leaves sizzled, the land hardened, the sun erased the rocks. There were no tablets or glyphs now—only disconnected stones, each as blank as a blank page.

I collected my gear and set off the way I'd come. The Road of the Gods seemed long, empty and long. By the time I reached the little museum, I had to stop to apply more suntan lotion. My guide had gone. By the time I reached the bus stop, I was ready to guzzle about two dozen soft drinks.

I was early. I found a boulder to sit on until the bus came. The ruins were not visible from here. I saw a rooster strutting alongside a rusted fence, as if he were doing guard duty; a pair of male and female turkeys were saying something in turkey language to each other, which, could they possess self-consciousness, possibly had been "I love you" or "Scram"; a hen with five tiny chicks in assorted colors pecked at the ground near a road sign.

Several bikers rode by; they carried firewood tied in bunches on the backs of their bicycles, and hunting rifles over their shoulders. A group of men hanging out beside a beat-up truck smiled in my direction; when they drove off, they waved, and honked the horn.

A few Indians stood on the opposite side of the highway, near the dirt road that led to the ruins. They never looked at me, nor smiled nor waved. They seem to have a trick of turning off the mind in such situations to make time vanish. It looks like mindlessness, but it is not. They turn off the conceptualizing part of the brain, but they remain perceptually awake—they have to, in a land and a country full of threat. It may be a knack for being sensorially aware without having to talk to themselves about what it is they are aware of that accounts for the Indians' frequent long silences: if you do not talk to yourself, you have less need to tell anyone else what you feel or think; you feel and think without naming yourself as feeler and thinker. It follows, then, that they may be closer to God, any god, but I can't say. If they aren't, they haven't told me. If they are, can they say?

Or maybe I was merely suffering from cultural shock, as real but transitory as the physical shock that had started my journey.

But suppose silence does bring us closer to God? I mean the inner silence of a language that does not refer to the self, that does not divorce the "I" from the "Thou" or even the "me." Would that be union, or would it signify the loss of the possibility of love? Is love predicated on divorce?

These are fundamental questions, and we are doomed to ask them. Yet it may be that the very asking of the questions precludes an answer. We cannot ask them without creating ourselves in our own image; we must use a reflexive language. Will our words make right turn after right turn forever, as if we were following correctly a map that can lead us nowhere? Is this an epistemological cul-de-sac?

We cannot know. It may be that it cannot pay off—it may be that the exercise is a futile one—but what we do know is that our disgraced and human condition means that from here on out we have no choice but the making of many books, books without end. This conclusion, though surprising, is logically unavoidable. If there are answers to be learned, they can be learned only in places where there is writing.